TRUTH MATTE

FOR YOU AND TOMORROW'S GENERATION

MW01001193

Josh McDowell

Managing Writer
Dave Bellis

Writers
Larry Keefauver
Bob Hostetler

World Bridge Press
127 Ninth Avenue, North
Nashville, Tennessee 37234

Reprinted 1996, 1997.

Distributed to the trade by Broadman and Holman Publishers.

ISBN: 0-8054-9834-6
Dewey Decimal Classification: 248.84
Subject Heading: TRUTH/ADULTS–RELIGIOUS LIFE

Unless indicated otherwise, Scripture quotations
are from the Holy Bible, *New International Version*,
© 1973,1978,1984 by the International Bible Society.

Printed in the United States of America

World Bridge Press
127 Ninth Avenue, North
Nashville, Tennessee 37234

Acknowledgments

I want to thank and humbly acknowledge a number of people who brought this project together. If not for their vision, dedication, and talent, this Workbook and its Leaders Guide simply would not have been published. I acknowledge:

• Jimmy Draper, Gene Mims, and Chuck Wilson with the Baptist Sunday School Board, and Broadman & Holman for their vision and commitment to the Right From Wrong message and campaign.

• John Kramp for his skilled leadership, publishing vision for the *Right From Wrong* workbooks, and his untiring efforts as he championed this project on behalf of the publisher.

• Dave Bellis, my associate of 18 years, for directing every aspect of the Right From Wrong Campaign, and being managing writer of this project, developing and focusing the content, and developing each product within the campaign into a coordinated package.

• Larry Keefauver for his insights, unselfish devotion, and writing skills as he translated the Right From Wrong message into the workbook format.

• Bob Hostetler for correlating and editing the Right From Wrong youth workbook outline and content into this workbook and for his witty and humorous writing style that brings a smile to every reader's face.

• Jimmy Hester, Debbie Colclough, and Joyce McGregor for their insights, educational design skills, and editing expertise as they readied the manuscript for publication.

Josh McDowell
Spring, 1995

Contents

The Absolute Truth • relativism • subjective and situational "truth" • objective, universal, and constant moral standards • the two models of truth • absolute truth

The Truth Process • the Truth process • the distinction between precept, principle, and person • immediate gratification • provision and protection

The 4Cs • the 4Cs: consider, compare, commit, count

The Honest Truth • honesty is rooted in the nature of the God of Truth • long-term benefits of God's protection and provision outweigh the short-term pleasure of dishonesty • honesty begins in a relationship with a young person

The Love Connection • right conduct in interpersonal relationships is rooted in the nature of the God of love • long-term benefits of God's protection and provision outweigh the short-term appeal of unloving actions and attitudes • we must admit our unloving attitudes and behaviors and submit to God's way of relating to others

The Urge to Merge • right sexual behavior (vs. wrong sexual behavior) is defined by the nature of God Himself • only sex that is characterized by love, purity, and faithfulness conforms to God's standard • long-term benefits of God's protection and provision far outweigh the short-term appeal of sexual immorality

The Stand • three pillars of "truth-telling" • truth and tolerance

Introduction

Read this first!

What do you consider the strangest animal on earth? The emu, the flightless, swift-running Australian bird? The manatee, the spoon-tailed warm-water mammal? The octopus? The chameleon? The jellyfish?

Well, in many ways, the book you hold in your hand is a strange animal, indeed. You are looking at a unique publishing venture and a dynamic reading adventure. *Truth Matters* is based on the largest known survey of churched youth (nearly 4,000 young people from 13 Christian denominations) ever conducted. This study is part of a multi-faceted campaign designed to restore biblical values and views to an entire generation. *Truth Matters* is an inductive, interactive workbook on a subject of great importance and urgency.

Truth Matters is designed to lead you on an eight-week journey of discovery. You'll discover many things you might not have known—things about truth, things about God, things about yourself, things about children and youth. You may not like everything you discover, but you will find it challenging, enlightening, and life-changing.

Truth Matters corresponds closely to the Right From WRong youth workbook, *Setting You Free to Make Right Choices* and the children's workbook *Truth Works!*. Many examples and illustrations are teen-oriented; a few employ younger children. This is purposeful; if the youth and children in your church are using the Right From Wrong workbooks their journey of discovery will correspond closely to yours, providing rich opportunities for discussion and reinforcement.

The integration of the youth and children's materials into *Truth Matters* will also help you identify the issues with which children or teenagers are struggling, and offer insight and suggestions on dealing with those issues. In addition, you will find that the principles, regardless of the age group employed in the illustrations, apply to individuals of any age ... even adults!

To get the most out of this workbook, set aside a specific time every day to study each day's assignment; each assignment will usually take from 25 to 30 minutes. Take your time; don't try to jump ahead, or complete several days' assignments in one sitting. Also, don't skip any assignments; each day builds on the previous day's discovery and leads to the next, so skipping over a day or two will rob you of crucial understanding and insight.

This study is also designed to be used in connection with weekly group sessions that will help clarify or amplify your understanding of the concepts you learn in the workbook. Be as faithful as possible to the group sessions, and you will reap even greater rewards from your personal study.

You're on the verge of a learning experience that could very well change your life and the lives of those you love. As you apply yourself to this material, may God apply the material to you.

How to Use Your Workbook

You are about to begin an exciting journey of learning how to teach your children and youth a process for making right choices that is based on God's nature and Word. This study is for adults who have significant relationships with children and youth as their parents, guardians, teachers, coaches, pastors, youth leaders, children's leaders, or friends. To gain the most from this study you will need to do the following.

In Your Personal Study
1. For your daily work in this workbook, you will need pencil, additional paper, and a Bible. Complete all written work on a daily basis.
2. Each week do the suggested assignments to help you begin to put into action what you've learned. These assignments are located on the unit page for the week.
3. Conclude each week with the weekly journal. You need not complete every statement in the weekly journal, but you should complete several statements.
4. Don't wait until you've completed all seven weeks of the workbook before working with your young person on what you have learned; begin right away honestly and openly to share your discoveries with those you love and care about. There's no time like the present to begin passing on sound biblical values to the children and youth in our lives.
5. Read Josh McDowell's book, *Right From Wrong*. If your local bookstore does not carry it, ask them to order a copy for you. Use the ordering information on pp. 9-12.

Memorizing Scripture

Memorizing Scripture is an important discipline you will be called on to use in your study. Consider the following ideas to help you further develop Scripture memorization.

1. Read the verse and think about the meaning.
2. Write the verse on notecards, one phrase per card.
3. Glance at the first phrase and say it aloud. Glance at the next phrase and say both phrases aloud. Continue this process until you have said the whole phrase.
4. Try to say the verse from memory later in the day. If you cannot remember the complete verse, glance at the cards to refresh your memory.
5. Repeat the verse several times each day for a week until you feel that the verse is firmly implanted in your mind.

In Preparation for Group Sessions

1. Attend all of the group sessions. You have probably received this workbook at the first group session. Each week you will need to do all of that week's activities and assignments before the group session. This is your schedule.

Before Group Session ...	complete in your workbook...
2,	Week 1: The Absolute Truth.
3,	Week 2: The Truth Process.
4,	Week 3: The 4Cs.
5,	Week 4: The Honest Truth.
6,	Week 5: The Love Connection.
7,	Week 6: The Urge to Merge.
8,	Week 7: The Stand.

2. Be certain to take your workbook to every group session along with pencil, paper, and your Bible. Your workbook includes the worksheets you will use during the group sessions.
3. Invite others to join you in this study. If you're married, do this study with your spouse. Encourage your church to start other groups with the video series or this curriculum study.
4. If you have not already viewed the *Truth Matters* video series by Josh McDowell, plan to do so as soon as this study is completed. Ask your group leader to order this series for your group and for the church.

Passing on the Truth to Our Next Generation

The "Right From Wrong" message, available in numerous formats, provides a blueprint for countering the culture and rebuilding the crumbling foundations of our families.

Read It and Embrace a New Way of Thinking

Right From Wrong, Trade Paper Book
ISBN 0-8499-3604-7

The Right From Wrong Book to Adults

Right From Wrong - What You Need to Know to Help Youth Make Right Choices
by Josh McDowell & Bob Hostetler

Our youth no longer live in a culture that teaches an objective standard of right and wrong. Truth has become a matter of taste. Morality has been replaced by individual preference. And today's youth have been affected. Fifty-seven percent (57%) of our churched youth cannot state that an objective standard of right and wrong even exists!

As the centerpiece of the "Right From Wrong" Campaign, this life-changing book provides you with a biblical, yet practical, blueprint for passing on core Christian values to the next generation.

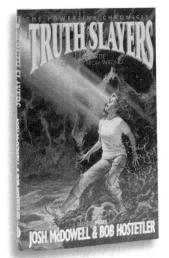

The Truth Slayers, Trade Paper Book
ISBN 0-8499-3662-4

The Truth Slayers Book to Youth

The Truth Slayers - The Battle of Right From Wrong
by Josh McDowell & Bob Hostetler

This book—directed to youth—is written in the popular NovelPlus format and combines the fascinating story of Brittney Marsh, Philip Milford and Jason Withers and the consequences of their wrong choices with Josh McDowell's insights for young adults in sections called "The Inside Story."

The Truth Slayers conveys the critical "Right From Wrong" message that challenges you to rely on God's word as the absolute standard of truth in making right choices.

Hear It and Adopt a New Way of Teaching

Right From Wrong, Audio–104 min.
ISBN 0-8499-6195-5

Right From Wrong Audio for Adults
by Josh McDowell

What is truth? In three powerful and persuasive talks based on the book *Right From Wrong*, Josh McDowell provides you, your family, and the church with a sound, thorough, biblical, and workable method to clearly understand and defend the truth. Josh explains how to identify absolutes and shows you how to teach youth to determine what is absolutely right from wrong.

See It and Commit to a New Way of Living

Video Series to Adults

Truth Matters for You and Tomorrow's Generation
Five-part Video Series featuring Josh McDowell

Josh McDowell is at his best in this hard-hitting series that goes beyond surface answers and quick fixes to tackle the real crisis of truth. You will discover the reason for this crisis, and more importantly, how to get you and your family back on track. This series is directed to the entire adult community and is excellent for building momentum in your church to address the loss of values within the family.

This series includes five video sessions, a comprehensive Leader's Guide including samplers from the five "Right From Wrong" Workbooks, the *Right From Wrong* book, the *Truth Slayers* book, and a 12-minute promotional video tape to motivate adults to go through the series.

Truth Matters, Adult Video Series
ISBN 0-8499-8587-0

Video Series to Youth

Setting You Free to Make Right Choices
Five-part Video Series featuring Josh McDowell

Through captivating video illustrations, dynamic teaching sessions, and creative group interaction, this series presents students with convincing evidence that right moral choices must be based on a standard outside of themselves. This powerful course equips your students with the understanding of what is right from what is wrong.

The series includes five video sessions, Leader's Guide with reproducible handout including samplers from the five "Right From Wrong" Workbooks, and the *Truth Slayers* book.

*Setting You Free to Make
Right Choices*, Youth Video Series
ISBN 0-8499-8585-4

Practice It and Make Living the Truth a Habit

Workbook for Adults

Truth Matters for You and Tomorrow's Generation
Workbook by Josh McDowell with Leader's Guide

The "Truth Matters" Workbook includes 35 daily activities that help you to instill within your children and youth such biblical values as honesty, love, and sexual purity. By taking just 25 - 30 minutes each day, you will discover a fresh and effective way to teach your family to make right choices—even in tough situations.

The "Truth Matters" Workbook is designed to be used in eight adult group sessions that encourage interaction and support ing. The five daily activities between each group meeting will help and your family make right choices a habit.

Truth Matters, Member's Workbook ISBN 0-8054-9834-6
Truth Matters, Leader's Guide ISBN 0-8054-9833-8

Workbook for College Students

Out of the Moral Maze
by Josh McDowell with Leader's Instructions

Students entering college face a culture that has lost its belief in absolutes. In today's society, truth is a matter of taste; morality of individual preference. "Out of the Moral Maze" will provide any truth-seeking collegiate with a sound moral guidance system based on God and His Word as the determining factor for making right moral choices.

Out of the Moral Maze, Member's Workbook with
Leader's Instructions
ISBN 0-8054-9832-X

Workbook for Junior High and High School Students

Setting You Free to Make Right Choices
by Josh McDowell with Leader's Guide

With a Bible-based emphasis, this Workbook creatively and systematically teaches your students how to determine right from wrong in their everyday lives–specifically applying the decision-making process to moral questions about lying, cheating, getting even, and premarital sex.

Through eight youth group meetings followed each week with five daily exercises of 20-25 minutes per day, your teenagers will be challenged to develop a life-long habit of making right moral choices.

Setting You Free to Make Right Choices, Member's Workbook
ISBN 0-8054-9828-1
Setting You Free to Make Right Choices, Leader's Guide
ISBN 0-8054-9829-X

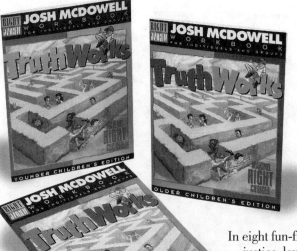

Workbook for Children

Truth Works - Making Right Choices
by Josh McDowell with Leader's Guide

To pass on the truth and reclaim a generation, we must teach God's truth when our children's minds and hearts are young and pliable. Creatively developed, "Truth Works" is two workbooks, one directed to younger chil-dren grades 1 - 3 and one to older children grades 4 - 6.

In eight fun-filled group sessions, your children will discover why such truths as honesty, justice, love, purity, self-control, mercy, and respect work to their best interests and how four simple steps will help them to make right moral choices an everyday habit.

Truth Works, Younger Children's Workbook ISBN 0-8054-9831-1
Truth Works, Older Children's Workbook ISBN 0-8054-9830-3
Truth Works, Leader's Guide ISBN 0-8054-9827-3

Contact your Christian supplier to help you obtain these "Right From Wrong" resources and begin to make it right in your home, your church, and your community.

The Absolute Truth

Imagine being approached by a friend at church.

"Hey," your friend says, "have you heard about the Club?"

"You mean that thing people put on their steering wheels so no one can steal their car?"

"No, I mean the new Club, the new organization the kids are all talking about."

"I haven't heard a thing," you answer.

"You've got to be kidding. I heard you already have a family membership."

"Not that I know of," you say.

"Well, you should find out, because membership can actually double a person's tendency to get drunk or steal, and triple the chances of getting involved in illegal drug use!"

"Why would I want to do that?" you ask, but your friend seems not to hear.

"And they say that children who join the Club become two times more likely to feel disappointed and resentful, two times more likely to lack purpose, and six times more likely to attempt suicide!"

Would you join a club like that? Would you want your children, grandchildren, or students involved in such a group? No? Well, believe it or not, children all around you may already be functioning members.

This week you will—
- discover more about the crisis of truth that faces the children and youth with whom you have relationships;
- begin to confront the crisis;
- understand the three characteristics of an acceptable standard of truth, and explore what moral standard meets those requirements;
- uncover the two models of truth that exist in our culture (and their effects upon us and our children and youth); and,
- clarify your understanding of what absolute truth is and how a cohesive view of truth can benefit you and the young people you love.

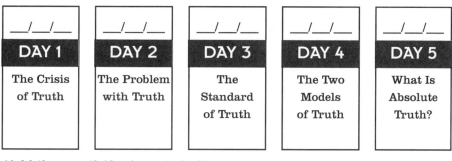

__/__/__	__/__/__	__/__/__	__/__/__	__/__/__
DAY 1	DAY 2	DAY 3	DAY 4	DAY 5
The Crisis of Truth	The Problem with Truth	The Standard of Truth	The Two Models of Truth	What Is Absolute Truth?

(Add the month/day/year to indicate when you complete your study.)

A key verse to memorize
"You will know the truth, and the truth will set you free" (John 8:32).

Concepts you will come to understand
- relativism
- subjective and situational "truth"
- objective, universal, and constant moral standards
- the two models of truth
- absolute truth

This Week's Assignments
- Memorize John 8:32.
- Complete daily exercises.
- Look for opportunities this coming week to gauge what standards you and the children and youth in your life are using to measure right and wrong. Be alert to opportunities presented by television shows, songs, comments, and everyday occurrences (such as being cut off in traffic) to ask, "Was that wrong?" "Why was it wrong?" and even "What standard (culture, personal opinion, law, etc.) are you comparing it to?" Try to make every day a laboratory for the discovery of the moral standards you and others around you ordinarily use. Be sure in your conversations with youth to evaluate whether those standards are objective, universal, and constant, reminding yourself and others why those qualities are important. As you work through the daily assignments you will learn the meaning of *objective, universal,* and *constant.*
- Complete your Weekly Journal.
- If you have not already done so, obtain a copy of *Right From Wrong,* (Josh McDowell and Bob Hostetler, Word Publishing, 1994). This book will greatly aid your study by providing background information on the nature of the problems we face. The book is the basis for this study. We suggest you read two to three chapters per week during the study.

The Crisis of Truth

Sixteen-year-old Elizabeth Peña and fourteen-year-old Jennifer Ertman made the mistake of taking a shortcut.

It was 11:30 p.m. on a hot, steamy June night. The two friends had just left a party at a friend's house. They called home before they left, to tell their mothers they were on their way. They never made it.

Elizabeth and Jennifer cut through a wooded area near the White Oak Bayou in Houston, Texas, and stumbled into an initiation ritual of the "Black N White" gang. Gang members had descended on the isolated area to drink beer and engage in a macho induction that involved the gang's newcomers fist-fighting other members. The gang gathering had just begun to break up when the girls appeared on the scene.

"Let's get 'em," cried one of the gang members.

Elizabeth's and Jennifer's naked bodies were found four days later. They had been raped repeatedly. Both girls had been strangled; one with a belt, the other with a shoelace. Apparently the girls did not die quickly enough. A police spokesman reported, "To ensure that both of them were dead, the suspects stood on the girls' necks."[1]

The six gang members charged with the murders (police reported that all six participated in the rapes and murders) ranged in age from fourteen to eighteen years old. One of the gang members had appeared on a local television show the day before the murders; he hoisted a beer and boasted into the camera, "Human life means nothing." Another of the boys, upon hearing that they might be charged with murder, is reported to have exclaimed, "Hey, great! We've hit the big time!" (Right From Wrong, 3-4).

Members of the Club

Those gang members were not only members of the Black N White gang; they were members of "the Club" discussed in the introduction to this week's studies. And their "membership" was a key factor in their crime. Research indicates that membership in "the Club" makes a young person:
- 36% more likely to lie to a parent or other adult;
- 48% more likely to cheat on an exam;

- 2 times more likely to try to hurt someone physically;
- 2 times more likely to watch a pornographic film;
- 2 times more likely to get drunk;
- 2½ times more likely to steal;
- 3 times more likely to use illegal drugs;
- 6 times more likely to attempt suicide.

Membership in "the Club" will not only affect the behavior of the children and youth you care about; it will also affect their attitudes, making them:
- 65% more likely to mistrust people;
- 2 times more likely to be disappointed;
- 2 times more likely to be angry with life;
- 2 times more likely to lack purpose;
- 2 times more likely to be resentful.

Check the symptoms of crisis that you have personally encountered or know about with young people you know (or know about) in your family, community, school, or church.

❏ teen suicide   ❏ child abuse
❏ drug use/abuse   ❏ lying
❏ sexual activity   ❏ unwed pregnancy
❏ alcohol use/abuse   ❏ rebellion against authority
❏ theft   ❏ abortion
❏ drunk driving   ❏ fighting/violence
❏ rape/attempted rape   ❏ profanity/obscenity
❏ cheating   ❏ gang activity

The Entrance Exam

How can you find out if those you know in the next generation are members of "the Club"? How can you discover if they're in that vulnerable category we talked about earlier? How can you determine whether the young people you care so much about are more likely to feel disappointed and resentful than the students who sit next to them in school?

The answer is *truth*. The research upon which *Right From Wrong* is based discovered that a child or teenager's view of truth was the single most influential factor in determining the degree of his or her involvement in the behaviors and attitudes we have listed. Nearly 4,000 churched youth were asked to respond to the following statements about objective standards of truth and morality. Right now, read the statements. We will ask you later to answer the question posed in the second column.

The Entrance Exam

Statement	Agree?		
	Yes	No	Not Sure
1. There is no such thing as "absolute truth"; people may define "truth" in contradictory ways and still be correct.	___	___	___
2. Everything in life is negotiable.	___	___	___
3. Only the Bible provides a clear and indisputable description of moral truth.	___	___	___
4. Nothing can be known for certain except the things you experience in your life.	___	___	___
5. When it comes to matters of morals and ethics, truth means different things to different people; no one can be sure they have the truth.	___	___	___
6. What is right for one person in a given situation might not be right for another person who encounters that same situation.	___	___	___
7. God may know the meaning of truth, but humans are not capable of grasping that knowledge.	___	___	___

A person's reaction to those statements will reveal to what degree he or she is sold on the biblical view of right and wrong. Only nine percent of the churched youth we surveyed provided a "pro-truth" reply to all seven statements (yes to #3, no to all the others). In other words, more than nine out of ten churched youth are members, to one degree or another, of "the Club."

Truth and You

Each of the questions in the entrance exam reveals what a person believes about absolute truth. Only one of the questions uses that phrase, but all of them measure whether you believe truth is absolute or relative.

You see, some people believe in absolute truth; that is, they believe that there are some things that are true for all people, for all times, and for all places. Others, of course, don't accept an absolute standard of truth; they believe that all truth is relative, that the line between right and wrong is different for

everyone. They believe that people may define *truth* in contradictory ways and still be correct, that truth means different
things to different people, that what is right for one person in a
given situation might not be right for another person in that
same situation.

Complete the following statement Jesus made about truth.

> "You will _____ the truth, and the truth will
> _____" (John 8:32).

Review the "entrance exam" in the light of Jesus' words.
According to His words, how do you think Jesus would have
answered each question?

Now it's time for you to take the entrance exam. Go back and
mark your honest response by each statement.

How did you respond to the "entrance exam" and to Jesus'
words? Check one.
- ❏ I don't believe in absolute truth.
- ❏ I believe in absolute truth.
- ❏ I believe in absolute truth, but I don't know what the truth is.
- ❏ I guess I'm not sure what I believe.
- ❏ Other _____

[1]Michele Ingrassia, with Peter Annin, Nina Archer Biddle, and Susan Miller, "Life
Means Nothing," *Newsweek*, 19 July 1993, 16-17.

Reviewing Today's Study

- Take a few moments to review today's lesson. Did you discover anything new? ❑ Yes ❑ No   If so, what did you discover?

_____

_____

_____

- Does what you believe about truth affect your attitudes or behavior? ❑ Yes ❑ No   If so, how?

_____

_____

_____

- Based on the "entrance exam," do you know any children or youth who might be members of "the Club?" ❑ Yes ❑ No

- Based on the "entrance exam," do *you* qualify for membership in "the Club"? ❑ Yes ❑ No

- Close your study with a prayer, honestly talking to God about your discoveries today and asking Him to reveal the truth to you.

DAY TWO

The Problem with Truth

The problem with truth (and, ultimately, the reason most people end up joining "the Club") is not believing that truth exists, or even believing that it can be known. As Charles Sanders Peirce said, "Every man is fully satisfied that there is such a thing as truth, or he would not ask any question."

The problem most people have is not the problem of acknowledging the existence of absolute truth, but agreeing on an acceptable standard. In other words, the problem with truth is not, "Does it exist?" but "What is the standard of truth?"

For example, if you and a friend disagree about how to spell a word, what would you do? You would probably consult a dictionary; that is a standard you both accept.

If you were following a recipe, how would you determine how much is a "cup" of milk? You would probably use a measuring cup; that is an acceptable standard.

If you had to mark off the base paths for your son's or daughter's baseball team, how would you know how far apart to place the bases? You would probably check a rule book; that is an acceptable standard.

But the problem faced by the members of "the Club" is that they have no standard outside themselves by which to measure the rightness or wrongness of their actions. They are often disappointed or angry with life because they tend to believe that no such standard exists. They think that they alone decide what is right or wrong in every circumstance.

But aren't they right? After all, what kind of standard is there for making decisions about right and wrong? You can't measure out a cup of "right." There is no "dictionary" of right and wrong deeds. Even if we're willing to admit the existence of a standard outside ourselves, where do we look?

Standard Equipment

Anyone who's ever bought a car knows that there are some things that a car *must* have—standard equipment such as tires, a steering wheel, and an engine. Those things are the most basic equipment; without them, it's not a car, it's a piece of junk.

It's pretty much the same with finding a standard to help decide issues of right and wrong. A true standard must possess some basic equipment, or it's no standard at all—just a piece of junk.

Any standard that identifies what's right or wrong must, first of all, be *objective*. What does *objective* mean? (Circle one number.)

Objective:
  1. what lawyers say in a courtroom when they don't like something
  2. existing independently of individual thought or opinion
  3. an emotional feeling that something is right
  4. what he was of her affection

A true standard of right and wrong must be objective; it must exist independently of what you (or any other person) thinks or feels. Otherwise, right and wrong could change from person to person: you may consider stealing to be wrong, but your neighbor may not. In the absence of an objective standard of right and wrong, you have no basis on which to inform your neighbor that he should not swipe your large-screen TV with surround sound.

The second piece of equipment that a true standard of right and wrong must possess is that it must be *universal*. What does *universal* mean? (Circle one number.)

Universal:
  1. endorsed by a major Hollywood movie studio
  2. popular among faculty and students at institutions of higher learning
  3. acceptable and/or pleasing to everyone
  4. applies to all people everywhere

A true standard of right and wrong must be not only objective, but also universal; it must apply to all people in all places. If it did not, right and wrong may change from culture to culture or even from community to community. You may consider it wrong to abuse children, for example, but if a neighboring culture disagrees, who can say they're wrong? In the absence of a universal standard of right and wrong, you have no basis on which to inform your neighbors that it is wrong to treat their children—or yours—in despicable ways.

applies cross-culturally

Third, any standard that identifies what's right and wrong must be *constant*. What does *constant* mean? (Circle one number.)

Constant:
1. one of the twin Roman cities in what is now Turkey (the other was Inople)
2. does not change with time
3. the opposite of instant
4. a title of nobility, similar in rank to Duke and Earl

A true standard of right and wrong must be not only objective and universal, it must also be constant; it must be unchanging. Otherwise, right and wrong might be different from generation to generation, or even from day to day. For example, you may consider racism to be wrong, but if standards of right and wrong can change over time, then you cannot condemn the atrocities of Nazi Germany or the slavery of pre-Civil War America. In the absence of a constant standard, you have no hope of knowing from one minute to the next whether an act is right or wrong.

Write three times in the margin John 8:32, your Scripture memory verse. Are you beginning to understand the significance of Jesus' words?

"I Confess—She Did It!"

Read Genesis 3:1-13 below, the story of the first enrollment into "the Club." When God confronted Adam and Eve about their terrible choice, they each revealed the standards by which they were trying to measure their actions.

> [1]Now the serpent was more crafty than any of the wild animals the Lord God had made. He said to the woman, "Did God really say, 'You must not eat from any tree in the garden'?"
> [2]The woman said to the serpent, "We may eat fruit from the trees in the garden, [3]but God did say, 'You must not eat fruit from the tree that is in the middle of the garden, and you must not touch it, or you will die.' "
> [4]"You will not surely die," the serpent said to the woman. [5]"For God knows that when you eat of it your eyes will be opened, and you will be like God, knowing good and evil."
> [6]When the woman saw that the fruit of the tree was good for food and pleasing to the eye, and also desirable for gaining wisdom, she took some and ate it. She also gave some to her husband, who was with her, and he ate it. [7]Then the eyes of both of them were opened, and they realized they were naked; so they sewed fig leaves together and made coverings for themselves.
> [8]Then the man and his wife heard the sound of the Lord God as he was walking in the garden in the cool of the day, and they hid from the Lord God among the trees of the

garden. ⁹But the LORD God called to the man, "Where are you?"

¹⁰He answered, "I heard you in the garden, and I was afraid because I was naked; so I hid."

¹¹And he said, "Who told you that you were naked? Have you eaten from the tree that I commanded you not to eat from?"

¹²The man said, "The woman you put here with me—she gave me some fruit from the tree, and I ate it."

¹³Then the LORD God said to the woman, "What is this you have done?"

The woman said, "The serpent deceived me, and I ate."

To what standard did Adam compare himself (v. 12)? _____

_____

To what standard did Eve compare herself (v. 13)? _____

_____

Now read Genesis 3:16-24. Circle some of the consequences Adam and Eve faced because of their membership in "the Club."

¹⁶To the woman he said, "I will greatly increase your pains in childbearing; with pain you will give birth to children. Your desire will be for your husband, and he will rule over you."

¹⁷To Adam he said, "Because you listened to your wife and ate from the tree about which I commanded you, 'You must not eat of it,'

"Cursed is the ground because of you; through painful toil you will eat of it all the days of your life. ¹⁸It will produce thorns and thistles for you, and you will eat the plants of the field. ¹⁹By the sweat of your brow you will eat your food until you return to the ground, since from it you were taken; for dust you are and to dust you will return."

²⁰Adam named his wife Eve, because she would become the mother of all the living.

²¹The LORD God made garments of skin for Adam and his wife and clothed them. ²²And the LORD God said, "The man has now become like one of us, knowing good and evil. He must not be allowed to reach out his hand and take also from the tree of life and eat, and live forever." ²³So the LORD God banished him from the Garden of Eden to work the ground from which he had been taken. ²⁴After he drove the man out, he placed on the east side of the Garden of Eden cherubim and a flaming sword flashing back and forth to guard the way to the tree of life.

Adam and Eve's choice turned out so badly because neither of their standards was appropriate.

Reviewing Today's Study

How do you feel about the following statements? Check all that you agree with.
- ❏ I believe that absolute truth exists.
- ❏ I admit the existence of a standard outside myself by which to measure the rightness or wrongness of my actions.
- ❏ I recognize an acceptable standard of right and wrong.

How do you respond to the ideas and concepts you've encountered so far in this study? Check all that apply.
- ❏ I'm not buying them.
- ❏ I understand them.
- ❏ I'm resisting them.
- ❏ I have some reservations.
- ❏ I want to learn more.
- ❏ I'm struggling with them.
- ❏ I don't understand them.
- ❏ I agree with them.
- ❏ I agree with most of them.
- ❏ I'm excited by them.

In the margin, write any reservations or objections that you have about what you've studied so far. Be honest.

Solomon once prayed for "a discerning heart" so that he would be able to "distinguish right from wrong" (1 Kings 3:9). Close today's study with a prayer asking God to:
- help you understand any concepts you're struggling with;
- answer any objections or resistance you're feeling;
- grant you a discerning heart so you may distinguish right from wrong; and,
- give you opportunity to share your discoveries with the children and youth in your life.

The Standard of Truth

According to yesterday's study, an acceptable standard of right and wrong must have three characteristics. Do you recall what they are? (Look back to page 21 if necessary). Complete the statements below.

A true standard of right and wrong must be O_bjective___

A true standard of right and wrong must be U_niversal___

A true standard of right and wrong must be C_onstant___

That's quite a bill to fill. It's one thing to say that a true objective of right and wrong must possess those characteristics, but where—realistically speaking—can we hope to find such a standard?

Look at the following list of "standards" you or others may use to measure questions of right and wrong. Which of them meet all three requirements for a true standard of right and wrong? (Check all that apply.)

- ❏ Your conscience
- ❏ What your parents taught you
- ❏ A Sunday School lesson
- ❏ Your philosophy of life
- ❏ The Communist Manifesto
- ❏ A Josh McDowell book
- ❏ Public opinion
- ❏ The Bill of Rights
- ❏ Your culture
- ❏ The government
- ❏ Your horoscope
- ❏ Your pastor

Do any of those choices meet the criteria? If not, where do we look? Where can we find a standard that is:
- outside ourselves;
- above ourselves; or
- before and beyond ourselves?

God on the Stage

Back in the days of Julius Caesar, there was a Roman poet and playwright named Horace. Horace criticized the laziness of many playwrights of his day. He strongly criticized those writers who, every time a problem occurred in the plot of their play, brought in one of the many Roman gods to solve it. Horace instructed, "Do not bring a god on to the stage unless the problem is one that deserves a god to solve it" (*Right From Wrong*, 80-81).

The challenge of trying to distinguish right from wrong is one that deserves—in fact, demands—a God to solve it. It is impossible to arrive at an objective, universal, and constant standard of truth and morality without bringing God onto the stage. If an objective standard of truth and morality exists, it cannot be the product of the human mind (or it will not be objective); it must be the product of another Mind. If a universal rule of right and wrong exists, it must transcend individual experience (or it will not be universal); it must be above us all, something—or Someone—that is common to all humanity. If a constant and unchanging truth exists, it must reach beyond human timelines (or it would not be constant); it must be eternal.

Those things—the requirements for a standard of truth and morality—are found only in God. He is the source of all truth. God alone is the Standard we need.

Biblical writers expressed this belief throughout the Scriptures. Let's consider passages that support the requirements we have been talking about.

Circle the words or phrases in the verses below to indicate that God is the *objective* source of truth.

> He is the Rock, his works are perfect ... A faithful God who does no wrong, upright and just is he" (Deuteronomy 32:4).

> As for God, his way is perfect; the word of the Lord is flawless. ... For who is God besides the Lord? And who is the Rock except our God? (Psalm 18:30-31).

Circle the words or phrases in the verses below to indicate that God is the *universal* source of truth.

> The mountains melt like wax before the Lord, before the Lord of all the earth (Psalm 97:5).

> The Holy One of Israel is your Redeemer; he is called the God of all the earth (Isaiah 54:5).

> The Lord has established his throne in heaven, and his kingdom rules over all (Psalm 103:19).

Circle the words or phrases in the verses below to indicate that God is the *constant* source of truth.

> Do you not know? Have you not heard? The Lord is the everlasting God, the Creator of the ends of the earth. He will not grow tired or weary, and his understanding no one can fathom (Isaiah 40:28).

> Everything God does will endure forever; nothing can be added to it and nothing taken from it (Ecclesiastes 3:14).

You see, God's nature and character define truth. God defines what is right and what is wrong. But truth is not something God decides; it is something God is.

The basis of everything we call moral, the source of every good thing, is the eternal God who is outside us, above us, and beyond us. The reason some things are right and some things are wrong is because there exists a Creator, Jehovah God, and He is a righteous God.

- The reason we think that there are such things as "fair" and "unfair" is because our Maker is a just God.

- The reason love is a virtue and hatred a vice is because the God who formed us is a God of love.

- The reason honesty is right and deceit is wrong is because God is true.

- The reason chastity is moral and promiscuity is immoral is because God is pure.

God is the standard of truth. God is the standard we need.

Reviewing Today's Study

How do you respond to today's study? _____

_____

Do you find it easy or difficult to accept God as the only true standard for right and wrong? (Chart your response on the line below by placing an X on the continuum.)

|⊢———|———|———|———|———|———⊣|
easy   difficult

To what standard have you been comparing your behavior? Check the one response that is most prevalent.
- ❏ my own ideas of right and wrong
- ❏ my parents and what they taught me
- ❏ my friends and what they say
- ❏ my society and what it says
- ❏ my church and what it says
- ❏ other _____

Do you think this week's study will affect your actions and attitudes in the future? ❏ Yes ❏ No

If so, in what way(s)? _____

_____

Spend a few moments in prayer, responding to what you have learned this week. Close by speaking or singing the following benediction:

Now to the King eternal, immortal, invisible, the only God, be honor and glory for ever and ever. Amen (1 Timothy 1:17).

The Two Models of Truth

DAY FOUR

Once upon a time, children were raised in an atmosphere that communicated absolute standards for behavior: certain things were right and certain things were wrong. A child's parents, teachers, ministers, youth workers, and other adults collaborated in an effort to communicate that the former should be heeded and the latter should be avoided. At one time, our society, by and large, explained the universe, humanity, and the purpose of life from the Judeo-Christian tradition: a belief that truth existed, and everyone could know and understand it. A clear understanding of what was right and wrong gave society a moral standard by which to measure crime and punishment, business ethics, community values, character, and social conduct. It became the lens through which society viewed law, science, art, and politics—the whole of culture. It provided a cohesive model that promoted the healthy development of the family, united communities, and encouraged responsibility and moral behavior (*Right From Wrong*, 12-13).

That paragraph from *Right From Wrong* paints a picture of "the way we were." But it doesn't reflect the world in which today's generation is growing up. That's because a major shift has occurred in people's thinking in recent generations, a shift involving two distinct models of truth, two ways in which people today view right and wrong. One view is held by those who are members of "the Club" and the other is held by those outside "the Club." They reflect two opposite ways of looking at the world:

   Model 1: Truth is defined by God for everyone;
   truth is objective and absolute.

   Model 2: Truth is defined by the individual;
   truth is subjective and situational.

The first model acknowledges that God—not man—is central, that God is the source of all things, and that He rules over all. God is the repository of truth, the author and judge of right and wrong.

The second model places the individual in control of moral matters; because the standard is within the individual, it is particular to that specific person (subjective) and circumstance (situational). In other words, each person considers himself or herself the judge of whatever is right or wrong in any given circumstance. It is an anthropocentric model; that is, it is man-centered, not God-centered.

Believe it or not, the second model—a relativistic model—is the one many of our youth and a number of adults use today. It has shaped and molded their world view. It is the lens through which they view life's choices, and the basis on which they make life's decisions.

Which model of truth do you accept? ❏ Model 1 ❏ Model 2

Why did you choose that model?_____

Which model do you think the young people in your life accept? ❏ Model 1 ❏ Model 2

Why do you think that? _____

Write in the margin John 8:32. Say it aloud three times.

All About Eve

Most people have no trouble accepting an objective standard of truth in such areas as mathematics or spelling. But for some reason, many of us resist the idea of a standard outside ourselves when it comes to decisions about right and wrong.

Of course, resistance to the first model of truth is nothing new; it is almost as old, in fact, as the first model of truth itself.

Read Genesis 3:1-6 below.

> ¹Now the serpent was more crafty than any of the wild animals the LORD God had made. He said to the woman, "Did God really say, 'You must not eat from any tree in the garden'?"
> ²The woman said to the serpent, "We may eat fruit from the trees in the garden, ³but God did say, 'You must not eat fruit from the tree that is in the middle of the garden, and you must not touch it, or you will die.' "
> ⁴"You will not surely die," the serpent said to the woman. ⁵"For God knows that when you eat of it your eyes will be opened, and you will be like God, knowing good and evil."
> ⁶When the woman saw that the fruit of the tree was good for food and pleasing to the eye, and also desirable for gaining wisdom, she took some and ate it. She also gave some to her husband, who was with her, and he ate it.

In tempting the woman, did the serpent appeal to the first model of truth or the second model of truth?
   ❑ Model 1   ❑ Model 2

What was Eve's mistake?
   ❑ eating the fruit
   ❑ wanting to make her own decision about what was right or wrong
   ❑ believing in the second model of truth
   ❑ all the above

Eve was a member of "the Club!" The serpent persuaded her to believe that the standard of right and wrong was inside herself.

Do you ever act like Eve?
   ❑ Yes   ❑ No   If so, how?_____

_____

Reviewing Today's Study

How does Eve's story relate to you? _____

_____

_____

Do you find yourself wanting to accept or wanting to reject the point of today's study? ❑ Accept   ❑ Reject

Why are you reacting this way? _____

_____

Based on your answer to the above question, compose a brief prayer in the margin, explaining your feelings to God. Ask God to continue challenging you to accept the fact that He is the standard of right and wrong.

DAY FIVE

What Is Absolute Truth?

Much of what we have studied this week may seem elementary to you. You may possess a strong biblical, Judeo-Christian world view. But research shows, unfortunately, that that is no guarantee that your children, grandchildren, students, or other young friends share your view.

The research upon which Right From Wrong is based indicates that the foundations upon which many parents, pastors, and youth leaders attempt to build are crumbling. Traditional biblical concepts are eroding; a Judeo-Christian world view is being undermined. Most of our youth lack the most basic moral perspectives that previous generations took for granted. Many of our young people are struggling with the concept of truth and how they are to apply it to their own life and experience. Our kids are confused about what truth is and who defines it; they are uncertain about what truths are absolute and what makes them absolute. Consequently, they are making conditional decisions, choosing what seems to be the best alternative at the time, without reference to any fundamental set of precepts or underlying principles to guide their behavior.

Many of our youth simply do not understand or accept absolute truth —that is, that which is true for all people, for all times, for all places. Absolute truth is truth that is objective, universal, and constant.

Now, the lines that define right behavior in our families or communities are not always absolute. For example, I have established a curfew with my 13-year-old daughter, specifying what time she should be home after a football game. I have told her, "It is not good to stay out beyond 11:00 p.m." I have set a firm guideline to be followed. If she obeys the curfew, she is right; if she violates it, she is wrong. I want my daughter to consider curfew as a hard and fast rule. And, in most cases she does.

But should we consider that guideline—to be home by 11:00 p.m. after every football game—an absolute truth? No. It is not applicable to all people, at all times, in all places. Communities, states, and governments may create various ordinances, regulations, and laws that are to be obeyed, but they are not necessarily absolutes. Ordinances change, regulations expire, and some laws only apply in certain states. In fact, even the curfew rule for my daughter may change someday. An absolute truth, on the other hand, is objective, universal, and constant.

> If our children are going to learn how to determine right from wrong, they must know what truths are absolute and why. They need to know what standards of behavior are right for all people, for all times, for all places. They need to know who determines truth—and why (*Right From Wrong,* 16-17).

Vive la Différence

How might a suggestion or law, for example, differ from absolute truth? Take some time thoughtfully to answer the following questions, according to what you've discovered this week.

Is there a difference between a parent's curfew and absolute truth?
❑ Yes ❑ No Why or why not? _____

_____

Is there a difference between prohibitions against murder and absolute truth?
❑ Yes ❑ No Why or why not? _____

_____

Is there a difference between specific rules of etiquette and absolute truth?
❑ Yes ❑ No Why or why not? _____

_____

Is there a difference between traffic laws (such as driving on the right side of the road) and absolute truth?
❑ Yes ❑ No Why or why not? _____

_____

Is there a difference between the Ten Commandments and absolute truth?
❑ Yes ❑ No Why or why not? _____

_____

Is there a difference between a person's taste in music and absolute truth?
❑ Yes ❑ No Why or why not? _____

_____

If you answered yes to any of the previous questions, do you think those things that are not absolute truths should be ignored?

❏ Yes   ❏ No   Why or why not? _____

_____

Is there a purpose, then, of clearly understanding what truths are absolute and why?

❏ Yes   ❏ No   Why or why not? _____

_____

Why Truth Matters

You may say that all this talk about absolutes seems abstract. But remember, abstract or not, the research shows that children's views about truth will really make a difference in their behavior. The research indicates that when our youth do not accept an objective standard of truth they become:

- 36% more likely to lie to you as a parent!
- 48% more likely to cheat on an exam!
- 74% more likely to watch MTV!
- 2 times more likely to try to hurt someone physically!
- 2 times more likely to watch a pornographic film!
- 2 times more likely to get drunk!
- 2½ times more likely to steal!
- 3 times more likely to use illegal drugs!
- 6 times more likely to attempt suicide!

If youth fail to embrace truth as an objective standard that governs their lives, the study shows it will make them:

- 65% more likely to mistrust people!
- 2 times more likely to be disappointed!
- 2 times more likely to be angry with life!
- 2 times more likely to be lacking purpose!
- 2 times more likely to be resentful!

How our youth (and for that matter, their parents and other adults) think about truth has a definite affect on their behavior—the choices they make, and the attitudes they adopt.

The following table makes it clear that many of our youth have no choice but to make conditional decisions—choosing what seems to be best in any given instance—without referring to the truth that God has revealed to us. "It appears," says [George] Barna, "that expecting today's youth to live in awareness of and accordance with a group of moral absolutes is unrealistic at this time."

Such a circumstance presents us with a challenge: to equip our youth with a belief in biblical truth that can guide their decisions and behavior, leading them to choose right in a world that so often encourages wrong choices.

Reactions to Statements About Absolute Truth

Statement	Agree	Disagree	Not Sure
1. Only the Bible provides a clear and indisputable description of moral truth.	72%	12%	16%
2. What is right for one person in a given situation might not be right for another person who encounters that same situation.	71%	15%	14%
3. When it comes to matters of morals and ethics, truth means different things to different people; no one can be absolutely positive they have the truth.	48%	29%	23%
4. Nothing can be known for certain except the things that you experience in your life.	39%	38%	23%
5. God may know the meaning of truth, but humans are not capable of grasping that knowledge.	31%	44%	25%
6. There is no such thing as absolute truth; people may define truth in contradictory ways and still be correct.	29%	43%	28%
7. Everything in life is negotiable.	23%	56%	21%
All 7 statements: Took a pro-truth position.	9%	91%	

(*Right From Wrong*, p. 265)

But what is it about truth that affects behavior? It works like this. When you believe an objective standard exists for distinguishing right from wrong—that certain things are right for all people, for all times, in all places—you acknowledge that there are fundamental moral and ethical guidelines that exist independently of your personal opinion. You acknowledge that the distinction between right and wrong is objective, universal, and constant. When you accept an objective standard for truth, you adopt a moral and ethical viewpoint that guides your choices of what is right and what is wrong. Your "truth view" acts as a lens through which you see all of life and its many choices. When our children and youth are equipped with the proper "truth view," they will be better able to identify what truths are absolute and what makes them absolute ... and they will have the equipment to make the right choices.

In our memory verse, John 8:32, Jesus states that one benefit of knowing the truth is that a Christian can be set free. What may be some other benefits of a sound understanding of truth? Circle in the following verses other benefits of a sound understanding of truth.

> Let love and faithfulness never leave you; bind them around your neck, write them on the tablet of your heart. Then you will win favor and a good name in the sight of God and man (Proverbs 3:3-4).

> Do not withhold your mercy from me, O Lord; may your love and your truth always protect me (Psalm 40:11).

> Send forth your light and your truth, let them guide me; let them bring me to your holy mountain, to the place where you dwell (Psalm 43:3).

> May he be enthroned in God's presence forever; appoint your love and faithfulness to protect him (Psalm 61:7).

> But we ought always to thank God for you, brothers loved by the Lord, because from the beginning God chose you to be saved through the sanctifying work of the Spirit and through belief in the truth (2 Thessalonians 2:13).

> Sanctify them by the truth; your word is truth (John 17:17).

Once we have helped the young people in our lives understand that truth exists, that it can be known, and that it will affect our happiness and satisfaction in life, the next question becomes, "How do I discern what things are right for all people, for all places, for all time?" Next week's study will answer that question.

Reviewing Today's Study

Are you enjoying the benefits of the truth in your own life?
❏ Yes ❏ No Why or why not?

_____

_____

What can you do this week—today, perhaps—to bring those benefits into your life?

_____

_____

Begin today to help the children and youth in your life begin to understand better and accept the truth. List ways you will do this.

_____

_____

Close today's study in prayer, confessing and committing to God all of your struggles and concerns. Ask Him to prepare you for the coming group session.

The Weekly Journal

The following page contains the first of seven opportunities in this study for you to reflect on what you are experiencing. You do not need to complete every statement, but you should complete several statements. When you arrive at the end of your seven-week journey through *Truth Matters,* you will be able to reflect on your personal growth and the challenges you faced along the way.

WEEKLY JOURNAL

I learned that _____

_____

_____

One attitude I had which changed was _____

_____

_____

God spoke to me by _____

_____

_____

One behavior that I will examine is _____

_____

_____

When I shared with the child or youth in my life, _____

_____

_____

The most difficult thing was _____

_____

_____

It was a joy to _____

_____

_____

Tomorrow I will _____

_____

_____

My Scripture memory verse is _____

_____

The Truth Process

Some time ago, I took my thirteen-year-old daughter, my seventeen-year-old son, and his girlfriend to see Stephen Spielberg's movie, *Schindler's List*. As we left the theater, we were surrounded by a somber crowd, many of whom were commenting on the atrocities inflicted upon the Jews by the Nazis. I turned to my son. "Sean," I said, "do you believe the holocaust was wrong—morally wrong?" He answered quickly. "Yes."

Then, as we got into the car to travel to a nearby town for dinner, I pursued the matter. "Almost everyone walking out of that theater would say the holocaust was wrong," I said. "But what basis would they have for making that judgment? Could they answer *why* it was wrong?"

I could see the wheels in three teenage minds spinning as I continued. "Most people in America subscribe to a view of morality called 'cultural ethics.' In other words, they believe that whatever is acceptable in that culture is moral; if the majority of people say a thing is 'right,' then it is right."

At about that time, we arrived at the restaurant and continued the discussion over dinner. "That's why many Americans will say that abortion is OK, because the majority of Americans—and Congress and the Supreme Court—have accepted it. If the majority thinks it's OK, it must be OK, right?

"But there's a problem with that," I explained. If that is true, then how can we say the 'aborting' of six million Jews in the holocaust was wrong? In fact, the Nazis offered that very argument as a defense at the Nuremberg Trials. They argued, 'How can you come from another culture and condemn what we did when our culture said it was acceptable?' In condemning them, the world court said that there is something beyond culture, above culture, that determines right and wrong."

I also went on to explain that most of what people call morality today is simply pragmatism. "If we don't condemn what the Nazis did," people reason within themselves, "what's to stop someone from doing it to us?" And they're right, of course; they recognize the need for objective morality, but they cannot arrive at a true moral code—because they refuse to acknowledge the original.

Finally, after about two hours at the restaurant, I thought it was time to guide those three teens to a discovery. "Do you know *why* what you saw tonight was wrong?" "I know it was wrong," Sean ventured, "but I don't know why." "There is a truth," I said, "that is outside me, above our family and beyond any human–a truth about killing that originates in God. Killing is wrong because there is a God and that God is a living God, who created life and said, 'It is good,' and commanded us to preserve life and not to kill" (*Right From Wrong*, 92-94).

In that conversation, Josh identified three keys to making right choices, three parts of a process that will help you make right choices. It is that process we will be discovering the next few days.

This week you will—
- learn how to trace the truth to the Standard (God) through the Truth process;
- discover how truth is often obscured because of the lure of immediate gratification; and
- equip yourself with an understanding of God's loving motivation in making His truth known to us.

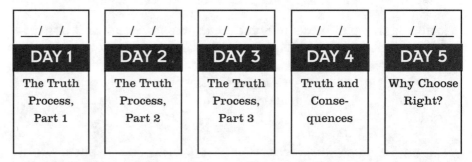

__/__/__	__/__/__	__/__/__	__/__/__	__/__/__
DAY 1	**DAY 2**	**DAY 3**	**DAY 4**	**DAY 5**
The Truth Process, Part 1	The Truth Process, Part 2	The Truth Process, Part 3	Truth and Consequences	Why Choose Right?

(Add the day/month/year to indicate when you complete your study.)

A key verse to memorize
"If you are pleased with me, teach me your ways so I may know you" (Exodus 33:13).

Concepts you will come to understand
- The Truth process
- The distinction between precept, principle, and person
- Immediate gratification
- Protection and Provision

This Week's Assignments

- Memorize Exodus 33:13.
- Complete daily exercises.
- Look for "teaching moments" in your interaction with children and youth this week in which to relate the precept-principle-person process. Such moments may happen when you are:
  - listening to a popular song together
  - at the mall
  - watching television or a movie together
  - riding in the car
  - discussing personal struggles or worries
  - at a sporting event
  - paying for a purchase at a cash register
  - helping your child or teenager do homework
- Take advantage of a shopping trip to discuss immediate gratification vs. long-term benefits with your child or teenager. For example, you may ask whether it's better to buy a cheap pair of tennis shoes or save up for a pair that will last longer. That discussion may open the door of opportunity for you to contrast the difference between short-term and long-term benefits.
- Complete your Weekly Journal.

DAY ONE

The Truth Process, Part 1

It's horrifying. It can sneak up on you unexpectedly. It can happen at the grocery store, at the dinner table, on the street, even in church.

You could be teaching Sunday School or driving a carload of children to a soccer game, when suddenly a strange force seems to take over your body, your mouth opens, and—oh, horrors!—you hear your parents' words coming out of your mouth!

"I've been worried sick about you," you may say. Or, "I don't know how you can find anything in that pigpen you call a bedroom."

Parents often say the strangest things. It can be surprising to hear yourself repeating the same phrases your mother or father used. But it shouldn't worry you too much; it happens to all of us, whether we're parents, teachers, pastors, or youth leaders. How many of the following phrases do you recall hearing from your parents? Check them.

❑ "If you keep crossing your eyes, they're going to stick like that!"
❑ "Don't look at me in that tone of voice!"
❑ "Don't listen to what I say, listen to what I mean."
❑ "This is going to hurt me more than it'll hurt you."
❑ "Do you think I enjoy cleaning up after you?"
❑ "Children are starving in India, and you can't even finish your brussels sprouts!"
❑ "Do you want me to give you something to cry about?"
❑ "When I was your age …"
❑ "I hope when you have children, they act just like you."
❑ "If I've told you once, I've told you a thousand times …"
❑ "Money doesn't grow on trees."
❑ "Talking to you is like talking to a brick wall."

Some of those phrases sound familiar, don't they? How many have you found yourself saying as an adult? It seems like every parent in the world has said those things at one time or another. You may not remember, but there are other phrases your parents have probably said repeatedly to you. See how many you can complete.

1. "Don't play with _____."

2. "Look both ways before you _____."

3. "Don't touch a hot _____."

4. "Say please and _____."

5. "Don't run with _____ in your hand."

6. "Don't sit too close to the _____. You'll ruin your eyes."

(Answers: 1. matches 2. cross the street 3. stove 4. thank you 5. scissors/knives/ sharp objects 6. TV)

These little exercises are mostly for fun, and you may be smiling as you complete them. But what's the point?

Each of the phrases in the second set is a precept. When you were a child, the communication between you and your parents was mostly in the form of precept. They repeatedly told you "do this," and "don't do that." As an adult, whether or not you are a parent, much of your interaction with the younger generation—particularly young children—is probably in the form of precept: "Be home by eleven o'clock," "Raise your hand if you want to speak," or "Don't run in the sanctuary."

The Precepts of the Lord

Similarly, God has issued precepts—we usually call them commands—to His people. God has told us, "do this," and "don't do that" in language as clear as your telling a child to "look both ways before you cross the street."

Read the Bible verses below and circle key words or phrases in each precept.

You shall have no other gods before me (Exodus 20:3).

Do not judge, or you too will be judged (Matthew 7:1).

Do not steal. Do not lie. Do not deceive one another (Leviticus 19:11).

It is God's will that you should be holy; that you should avoid sexual immorality (1 Thessalonians 4:3).

You shall not murder (Deuteronomy 5:17).

A new command I give you: Love one another. As I have loved you, so you must love one another (John 13:34).

Obey your leaders and submit to their authority. They keep watch over you as men who must given an account. Obey them so that their work will be a joy, not a burden, for that would be of no advantage to you (Hebrews 13:17).

The precepts above are just a few of the commands God gives in His Word. (Jewish tradition maintains that God gave 627 specific commands!)

God has communicated a lot about Himself to us through precepts. God's commands reveal what He likes, what He doesn't like, what He considers important, what He thinks is good, and what He thinks is bad. But few people realize that precept—the rules, regulations, codes, and requirements of Scripture—is but the first step in understanding basic morality. The precepts of the Lord are not just a bunch of do's and don'ts, shalts and shalt-nots. They are designed also to lead us beyond the precept to the next step in the process of Truth.

Reviewing Today's Study

Complete the following sentences to express your response to today's study.

I'm feeling _____

_____

_____

I'm thinking _____

_____

_____

I'm having trouble _____

_____

_____

I'm starting to realize _____

_____

_____

God's speaking to me through His Word. He's saying _____

_____

_____

Take a few moments to respond in prayer to what God's Word is teaching you.

Lord, Your Word is showing me _____, and I want to respond by _____. Please help me to _____, and teach me Your ways, so that I may know You and find favor with You, and so that I may teach Your truth to the young people in my life. Amen.

DAY TWO

The Truth Process, Part 2

"You lied to me!" Amanda's mom said. She faced her daughter in the kitchen, a fist propped on each hip.

Amanda rolled her eyes. Her mother hated it when she did that. Her mom continued. "How could you lie to your own mother?"

"I had to, Mother," Amanda answered. "You would never have let me go to the party if I'd told you it was at Steve Hanson's house."

"You're right there, little lady." Sometimes her mother just couldn't figure out what was going on in her daughter's head. Amanda would turn sixteen in two weeks, and yet she still acted like a child.

"Why are you making such a big deal out of this?" Amanda said. "Nothing happened."

"I'm making a big deal out of it because it's wrong!"

"What was so wrong? I went to a fun party and you had a relaxing evening at home, without worrying about your 'little lady.' "

"What was so wrong? We've taught you better than that. Lying is wrong, Amanda Lynn." She always called her daughter by her full name when she was angry or exasperated, and she was both of those things now. She knew Amanda hated her middle name; she complained that it made her sound like a musical instrument, "a mandolin." That was just like Amanda, to complain because her name sounded musical.

"Why is it so wrong?" Amanda asked.

"Because it is," her mom answered. *What was wrong with her?* she wondered. Talking to Amanda could be like talking to a brick wall sometimes.

"Oh, that's just great, Mother. 'Because it is' is not a reason."

"Because the Bible says it's wrong," her mom countered.

Amanda responded without hesitation, "I told you, Mother—"

But before she could finish, her mom said, " 'Thou shalt not lie.' Sound familiar?"

"I had to say what I said, OK?" Amanda reasoned.

" 'Honor your father and your mother.' Sound familiar?"

"Why can't you just understand?"

There's a lot happening in that conversation. We can learn a lot about Amanda and her mother just from it. You may even have had a similar conversation with a young person. Amanda's mom has a point, of course. According to the precepts of the Lord, lying *is* wrong. But the precepts also point to something else, something further that we can know about right and wrong.

The Principles of Right and Wrong

Precepts point to larger principles in God's Word. While a precept is a specific rule or commandment, a principle is a broader application of numerous precepts. If all of God's commands are the first step toward knowing Him and distinguishing right from wrong, principles are the next step, because behind each precept is a principle.

A principle is a norm or standard that may be applied to more than one type of situation. To understand the difference between a principle and a precept, think of a principle as expressing the fundamental truth on which a precept is based....

Principles help explain the "why" behind a command. A concern for safety is one of the principles behind a mother's command to look both ways before crossing the street. As I explained to my children after we saw Schindler's List together, reverence for life is the principle behind the command, "Thou shalt not kill." A principle behind the command, "You shall not give false testimony," is honesty (*Right From Wrong*, 96).

Learning to identify the principles behind God's precepts will help us see the overarching truth that applies, even when a specific command doesn't seem to apply.

Write in the margin the Scripture memory verse, Exodus 33:13. Say it aloud three times. Be sure to include the reference as you repeat it. Ask God to help you commit this verse not only to memory but to your life.

Precepts and Principles

What is the principle—the *why*—behind God's command to "avoid sexual immorality" (1 Thessalonians 4:3)? What is the principle—the overarching truth—behind God's command, "Do not defraud your neighbor or rob him" (Leviticus 19:13)?

Write the letter of the principle in the blank to match the precept they expressed in each Scripture passage.

Principles
a. Purity   d. mercy   g. Justice
b. Respect   e. Self-control   h. Love
c. Honesty   f. Unity   i. Generosity

Principle   Precept

_____   1. You shall not steal (Exodus 20:15).

_____   2. Do not oppress an alien; you yourselves
                      know how it feels to be aliens, because
                      you were aliens in Egypt (Exodus 23:9).

_____   3. Give to the one who asks you, and do not
                      turn away from the one who wants to
                      borrow from you (Matthew 5:42).

_____   4. Children, obey your parents in the Lord,
                      for this is right (Ephesians 6:1).

_____   5. This is the message you heard from the
                      beginning: We should love one another
                      (1 John 3:11).

_____   6. Is it not to share your food with the hun-
                      gry and to provide the poor wanderer
                      with shelter—when you see him naked,
                      to clothe him, and not to turn away from
                      your own flesh and blood? (Isaiah 58:7).

_____   7. Nor should there be obscenity, foolish
                      talk or coarse joking, which are out of
                      place, but rather thanksgiving
                      (Ephesians 5:4).

_____   8. Flee from sexual immorality. All other
                      sins a man commits are outside his body,
                      but he who sins sexually sins against his
                      own body (1 Corinthians 6:18).

_____ 9. For this reason a man will leave his
father and mother and be united to his
wife, and they will become one flesh
(Genesis 2:24).

(Answers: 1., c.; 2., g.; 3., i.; 4., b; 5., h.; 6., d.; 7., e.; 8., a.; 9., f.)

Reviewing Today's Study

• What have you discovered as a result of this week's study?

_____

• Have you disobeyed today any of the precepts referenced?
This week? ❑ Yes ❑ No If so, which ones?

_____

• Which principles have you lived out today? This week?

_____

• Do you react differently to the precepts than you do to the
principles? ❑ Yes ❑ No If so, which ones?

_____

If so, why do you think that is? _____

_____

• What do you wish to say to God in response to today's
study? Write your response below, in the form of a prayer.

_____

_____

DAY THREE

The Truth Process, Part 3

Paul Harvey's voice has been recognizable to generations of radio listeners. His daily radio broadcasts feature crisp commentary and invariably conclude with a human interest story, containing his trademark line, "And that's the rest of the story."

Knowing God's precepts, and even the principles of truth that lie behind those precepts, is not the end of the story. The process of discerning truth—of distinguishing right from wrong—leads from precept, through principle, to the Person of God Himself. That's "the rest of the story."

Too many people focus on God's law, and never see what it teaches us about the character of God. The ultimate purpose of God in every precept is to bring us to the knowledge of Himself, because He desires a relationship with us. We can only know truth by knowing the God of truth.

You see, God's law is not an end in itself. Some of His commands are illustrative, others are practical, but all are an expression of God's character. Note in the spaces provided the qualities of God's commands which King David extolled in Psalm 19:7-9 (we printed it for you on p. 53).

The law of the Lord is _____,
 reviving the soul.
The statutes of the Lord are _____,
 making wise the simple.
The precepts of the Lord are _____,
 giving joy to the heart.
The commands of the Lord are _____,
 giving light to the eyes.
The fear of the Lord is _____,
 enduring forever.
The ordinances of the Lord are _____
 and altogether righteous.

Note carefully the words David used to describe God's law: *perfect, sure, right, radiant, pure,* and *righteous.* Why does the law possess those qualities?

_____

_____

The truth resides in the commands of God because those commands were given by the God of truth. The truth would not cease being true if the Law were to disappear from the face of the earth, nor would it cease to be true if there were no humans to discern the principle. The truth resides in the eternal person of God Himself.

We can more effectively determine right from wrong and pass it on to the next generation when we look to God's nature and character as the measure of truth and morality. We can help children and youth make right choices when we learn the process of truth ourselves, tracing the truth through the precept and principle to the person of God Himself.

Write in the margin the Scripture memory verse, Exodus 33:13.

Amanda's Second Chance

Remember Amanda, the girl who misled her mother so she could go to a party at a friend's house? Do you think Amanda's conversation with her mother might have turned out differently if her mother had been able to see beyond the precept, through the principle behind the command and, ultimately, to the person of God Himself?

Write a better ending to that scene.

"What was so wrong? I went to a fun party and you had a relaxing evening at home, without worrying about your 'little lady.'"

"What was so wrong? We've taught you better than that. Lying is wrong, Amanda Lynn." She always called her daughter by her full name when she was angry or exasperated, and she was both of those things now. She knew Amanda hated her middle name; she complained that it made her sound like a musical instrument, "a mandolin." That was just like Amanda, to complain because her name sounded musical.

"Why is it so wrong?" Amanda asked.

_____

_____

_____

_____

_____

_____

_____

_____

_____

_____

A pastor friend of mine has a son in college. He had just read the *Right From Wrong* book and was discussing some of the concepts with his son. He asked his son, "Would you abstain from sex before marriage?"

"Yes," came the quick reply.

"Why?" asked my friend.

"Because premarital sex is wrong," was his son's response.

"Why is it wrong?"

"Because I read the Bible, listened to you and Mom, and decided for myself to stay pure before marriage," the son proudly announced.

As much as my friend appreciated and commended his son's reply, he proceeded to explain that he thought his son's response fell short.

Why do you think the father was not completely satisfied with his son's answer?

_____

_____

We help children and youth determine right from wrong when we teach them to fear God and to look to His nature and character as the measure of truth and morality. We must make clear to them that an attitude or behavior is not wrong just because adults frown, stamp their feet, and say it's wrong. It's wrong if it is not like God, because His person defines truth. He is the God of truth (see Deuteronomy 32:4).

Reviewing Today's Study

- How do you respond in your heart when you're confronted with the precepts of the Lord?

_____

_____

- How do you respond in your heart when you're confronted with the principles behind those precepts?

_____

_____

- How do you respond in your heart when you're confronted with the person of God Himself?

_____

_____

- Do you understand any better today how learning "God's ways" can help you know Him and find favor with Him?
  ❑ Yes ❑ No Why or why not?

_____

_____

- Look again at Psalm 19:7-9 below. Use those verses as a guide for prayer. Praise God for the qualities the Law possesses (perfect, trustworthy, etc.). Pray through the verses again, praising God because those are His attributes as well.

  The law of the Lord is perfect, reviving the soul. The statutes of the Lord are trustworthy, making wise the simple. The precepts of the Lord are right, giving joy to the heart. The commands of the Lord are radiant, giving light to the eyes. The fear of the Lord is pure, enduring forever. The ordinances of the Lord are sure and altogether righteous.

DAY FOUR

Truth and Consequences

"Welcome to TV's most popular game show, in which contestants compete for fantastic awards and prizes!" [Wild shouts and applause from the studio audience as camera pans a brightly lit stage to the accompaniment of up-tempo theme music.]

"And now, ladies and gentlemen, the host of Truth and Consequences, Tom Foolery!" [More shouts and applause as handsome host jogs down the center aisle through the audience and leaps onto the stage, without mussing his hair.]

"Thank you, thank you, thank you." [Foolery smiles broadly, revealing two perfect rows of white teeth, and speaks without moving his lips.]

"It's time for our first contestants. Let's give a Truth and Consequences welcome to Paul and Susan!"

[Two people leap from their seats in the audience and jog down the aisle and up the steps to join Foolery on the stage. Foolery shoves a microphone under Susan's mouth.]

"Susan, tell us a little bit about yourself."

"Well, I'm a dental technician from Navajo, Idaho, and —"

"That's great, Susan!" [Foolery glances at Paul's name tag and points the microphone his direction.]

"Where are you from, Paul?"

"Hi, Tom. I'm from Tuscaloosa, Alabama." [Foolery smiles into the camera.]

"Well, Paul, if my Tuscaloosa, I'd get it tightened." [Riotous laughter wafts into the studio through loudspeakers. Foolery strides stage right, and motions for Susan and Paul to follow him.]

"Let's play *Truth and Consequences*. Our first game involves these two doors."

[He points to two large, brightly colored doors on the stage. He pulls an index card from his pocket and begins to read.] "You may choose the prize that's behind the red door or the prize behind the blue door. I'll even tell you what the prizes are." [The sound of a drum roll enters the studio through the loudspeakers.]

"Behind the red door are two free tickets to next Saturday's Counting Cannibals concert. A group of your friends is already going, and you want to go, don't you?" [Paul and Susan nod; the audience applauds.]

"But you don't have the money, do you?" [Paul and Susan nod again; the audience applauds.]

"Behind the blue door is a night at home alone watching reruns of *Matlock*."

"I choose the red door!" [The audience erupts in applause again as Paul and Susan simultaneously shout their response. Foolery flashes a toothy smile.]

"Not so fast. In order to open the red door, you must agree to 'borrow' sixty dollars from your friend's purse ... after all, you didn't think *we'd* buy the tickets, did you? And, of course, you can always repay the money later." [Laughter again wafts into the studio through the loudspeaker. Foolery continues speaking.]

"To open the blue door, simply don't 'borrow' the money. What'll it be, the concert of the year with all your friends ... or home alone with *Matlock*?"

Red Door, Blue Door

Rather clear cut choice, wouldn't you say? Based on what you know now about the precepts, principles, and person of the God of truth, how would you discern the rightness or wrongness of those two choices? How would you explain this to a young person?

_____

_____

Do you think your explanation would be sufficient to convince Paul and Susan to choose the blue door? Why or why not?

_____

_____

Tom Foolery's game illustrates the fact that, even when we measure right and wrong according to God's nature and character, it doesn't guarantee we will choose right. The battle isn't over when we *discern* what's right; we must still *do* what's right.

That's not always easy, however, especially for a child or teenager. Many wrong choices offer immediate gain, while right choices often seem to involve short-term pain. Sin is often packaged very appealingly and carries a promise of instant gratification. Right choices, on the other hand, often require postponing immediate satisfaction for better long-term results.

Pain or Gain?

To be honest, we need to admit to ourselves and to the younger generation that the right choice is not always the easiest. If immoral behavior held no promise of reward or gratification, we'd have no trouble making the right choice, would we? We must be candid about the fact that, if we make choices simply on the basis of what will bring immediate pain or gain, the wrong choice will often be the most attractive.

This dilemma isn't new to our generation; it's been going on for centuries. The following moral choices were made by biblical characters. Consider whether you think they were swayed by the promise of immediate gratification and what the results of their decisions were. Check one box in each column for each situation.

1. Read Genesis 3:1-24. When Eve ate the forbidden fruit and persuaded her mate to imitate her, she:
   - ❑ chose immediate gain
   - ❑ chose to endure immediate pain
   - ❑ enjoyed long-term benefits
   - ❑ experienced long-term consequences

2. Read Genesis 12:10-20. When Abraham lied to Pharaoh about Sarah being his sister, he:
   - ❑ chose immediate gain
   - ❑ chose to endure immediate pain
   - ❑ enjoyed long-term benefits
   - ❑ experienced long-term consequences

3. Read 2 Samuel 11-12. When David committed adultery with Bathsheba, he:
   - ❑ chose immediate gain
   - ❑ chose to endure immediate pain
   - ❑ enjoyed long-term benefits
   - ❑ experienced long-term consequences

4. Read Ruth 3-4. When Boaz treated Ruth in a pure and loving way, he:
   - ❑ chose immediate gain
   - ❑ chose to endure immediate pain
   - ❑ enjoyed long-term benefits
   - ❑ experienced long-term consequences

5. Read Matthew 1:18-25. When Joseph treated Mary with honor and dignity (though she was pregnant out of wedlock to him), he:
- ❑ chose immediate gain
- ❑ chose to endure immediate pain
- ❑ enjoyed long-term benefits
- ❑ experienced long-term consequences

Even today we find ourselves in similar situations. We are often tempted to choose immediate gain without considering the long-term consequences. Remember, right choices often require postponing immediate satisfaction for better long-term results.

Reviewing Today's Study

- With which of the biblical characters in today's study do you most identify?
  - ❑ Eve
  - ❑ Abraham
  - ❑ David
  - ❑ Boaz
  - ❑ Joseph

Why? _____

- Review the choices you have made today. Did you choose immediate gratification? Why or why not?

_____

- List five or more situations this week in which you or a young person in your life were faced with a moral choice.

1. _____

2. _____

3. _____

4. _____

5. _____

• In those situations, did you or that young person choose immediate gratification:
  ❏ all the time
  ❏ most of the time
  ❏ about half the time
  ❏ hardly ever
  ❏ never

• Since wrong choices so often seem to promise immediate "rewards," why would a person ever make the right choice?

_____

_____

• What can you say to God in response to what you've learned today? Write your response in the form of a prayer.

_____

_____

_____

• Write this week's memory verse, Exodus 33:13. _____

_____

Why Choose Right?

DAY FIVE

"Time's up!" [Truth and Consequences host Tom Foolery grins and raises his eyebrows. He addresses Paul and Susan.]

"What'll it be, kids? The red door…" [He sweeps his hand toward the red door.]

"Or the blue door?" [He waves at the blue door as if batting at a fly, and points the microphone at Susan.]

"I'll take the red door." [The audience applauds wildly. Foolery tips the microphone toward Paul.]

"Can I take the red door, too?"

"You sure can!" [Foolery's grinning expression hasn't changed.]

"Well, then, I want the red door, too!" [Audience claps and cheers, Foolery grins into camera, and theme music begins playing through the studio loudspeakers.]

"Congratulations, folks! You're going to the Counting Cannibals concert! And *we're* going to a commercial. We'll be back after these messages." [Fade and out.]

Who Wouldn't Choose Red?

That scenario is more realistic than you may think, as attested to by youth themselves.

> In speaking to thousands of youth all over the world, I will often call several teens and young adults onto the stage with me and ask them a series of questions.
>
> "Do you think lying is wrong?" I'll ask.
>
> Invariably the young person will answer, "Yes."
>
> Then I ask another question. "If you were in a situation in which telling a lie would bring immediate rewards, and *not* lying could have bad results, would you lie?"
>
> Usually the young person will answer immediately, "Yes." Sometimes I get the answer, "Probably." One time, a young woman wrinkled her brow, thought for a moment, and said, "I'd have to pray about it." (from Josh McDowell's *Right from Wrong* seminars)

Those youth are struggling with the tension between the immediate gain of wrong choices and the immediate pain of right choices. Their attitude might be phrased, "Given an option between a wrong choice that offers immediate rewards and a right choice that doesn't, why choose right?"

Fair question. In order to answer it for yourself and for the young people in your life, you have to realize that in such instances children, youth, and adults seldom consider all the relevant information.

You see, a lot of people—Christians included—see God's commands as constricting. They think that biblical morality is confining. People don't see the benefits to a moral lifestyle. But God's commands, like those of a loving parent—"don't touch the stove," "look both ways before you cross the street," "eat your vegetables"—are not meant to spoil our fun and make us miserable.

God gave commands, such as "Flee sexual immorality," and "Husbands, love your wives," "You shall not commit adultery," and all other commands because he wanted to protect us and provide for us. God didn't put those precepts in the Bible just because He liked the way they sounded; God didn't concoct those rules to be a killjoy or to throw His weight around. God gave those commands because He knew some things we didn't. He knew, for example, that sexual immorality is a path to emptiness and frustration, not to pleasure and fulfillment.

Consider what Moses said about God's commands according to Deuteronomy 10:12-13.

> [12]And now, O Israel, what does the LORD your God ask of you but to fear the LORD your God, to walk in all his ways, to love him, to serve the LORD your God with all your heart and with all your soul, [13]and to observe the LORD's commands and decrees that I am giving you today for your own good?

According to those verses, why did God issue His commands?

_____

_____

Looking down from an objective, universal, and eternal perspective, God could see things that we cannot, and He issued precepts to protect us and provide for us.

Read Jeremiah 29:11 below and answer the following questions.

"For I know the plans I have for you," declares the Lord, "plans to prosper you and not to harm you, plans to give you hope and a future."

1. Who knows the plans God has for you? _____

_____

2. What kind of plans are they? _____

_____

3. Does this verse refer to God's protection and provision?
   ❏ Yes   ❏ No   If so, how?

_____

_____

Next, read Jeremiah 32:39-41 below, in which God talks about what He desires for those who follow Him.

³⁹I will give them singleness of heart and action, so that they will always fear me for their own good and the good of their children after them. ⁴⁰I will make an everlasting covenant with them: I will never stop doing good to them, and I will inspire them to fear me. ⁴¹I will rejoice in doing them good and will assuredly plant them in this land with all my heart and soul.

1. Why does God want people to fear Him and obey Him?

_____

2. What does God rejoice in?_____

_____

3. Do these verses make it sound like God wants to spoil your fun or prevent you from enjoying the best life has to offer?
   ❏ Yes   ❏ No

Now, all this doesn't mean that bad things won't happen to moral people, or that immoral people are never happy. But God's commands mark the path to the greatest rewards.

For example, suppose Paul had chosen the blue door instead of imitating Susan's choice of the red door. She would have enjoyed the concert, and he would have spent the night alone watching *Matlock*. That might not seem so bad to you and me, but many young people would rather eat dirt than endure such a fate. But though they may not have been so immediately gratifying, think about the benefits of his choice. Choose one answer that best describes your response.

- Paul would not have had to worry about
  ❏ what other people might think of his choice.
  ❏ coming up with the money to repay his friends.
  ❏ paying the consequences for his decisions.

- Paul would not have had to wrestle with
  ❏ whether his decision was right or wrong.
  ❏ his relationship with his friends.
  ❏ going against God's desires.

- Paul would have been able to face his friends without
  ❏ feeling guilty.
  ❏ wondering if they knew that he had taken the money.
  ❏ worrying about paying them back.

- Paul would have bolstered his sense of
  ❏ self-worth.
  ❏ pride.
  ❏ godliness.

- Paul would have contributed to a pattern of behavior that could earn him a reputation as
  ❏ a person of integrity.
  ❏ an honest man.
  ❏ a fool.

Long after the Counting Cannibals concert was over, Paul could have been enjoying the benefits of honesty—if he had made the right choice.

The Long and Short of God's Protection and Provision

The research study that revealed the existence of "the Club" clearly supports the notion that immoral behavior produces negative results. It indicates that moral behavior makes kids more likely to say they are satisfied with their lives, that they have high hopes, that they are respected by others. The study seems to show that right choices breed a healthy self-esteem, making kids more likely to think of themselves as achievers.

Phrases Surveyed Youth Used to Describe Themselves

	accurate? Yes	No		accurate? Yes	No
a. too busy	54%	46%	n. have high hopes	87%	13%
b. stressed out	50%	50%	o. disappointed	35%	65%
c. optimistic	54%	46%	p. confused	55%	45%
d. content	59%	41%	q. always tired	46%	54%
e. lazy	41%	59%	r. religious	78%	22%
f. angry with life	26%	74%	s. lonely	36%	64%
g. skeptical	33%	67%	t. encouraged	74%	26%
h. upbeat	63%	37%	u. seeking answers	74%	26%
i. lacking purpose	20%	80%	v. resentful	25%	75%
j. unmotivated	21%	79%	w. reliable	86%	14%
k. physically attractive	61%	39%	x. an achiever	80%	20%
			y. respected by others	86%	14%
l. mistrust people	32%	68%	z. temperamental	47%	53%
m. high integrity	60%	40%			

(Right From Wrong, p. 259)

Immoral behavior, on the other hand, fosters negative attitudes, making kids more likely to say they are *resentful, lonely, angry with life, unmotivated, disappointed,* and *confused.*

You see, when Jesus said, "You will know the truth, and the truth will set you free" (John 8:32), He spoke not only of the freedom *from* (freedom from things like disease, disillusionment, and disappointment), but also of freedom *to* (freedom to love and be loved, to trust, and to laugh). Being obedient to God's truths does not mean giving up the pleasures of sex and leisure, of satisfaction and liberty; it means being free to enjoy *maximum* sex, *maximum* leisure, *maximum* satisfaction, and *maximum* liberty, in the way that God intended (*Right From Wrong,* 111).

God provides lasting and eternal benefits when we make right choices. His provision may not be immediate, however. In fact, most often the wrong moral decision offers immediate benefits but results in long-term negative consequences. Likewise, making the right moral decision may result in short-term difficulties, suffering, or persecution; but God will provide and protect in the long run. Reflect on this a moment.

Reviewing Today's Study

- What could be some of the short-term benefits to lying? to stealing? to sexual immorality?

  _____

  _____

  _____

- What could be some of the long-term negative consequences to lying? stealing? to immoral behavior?

  _____

  _____

  _____

- What could be some of the short-term difficulties caused by telling the truth? not stealing? being pure and abstinent before marriage?

  _____

  _____

  _____

- What are some of the long-term benefits provided by God in being honest? not stealing? being pure and abstinent before marriage?

  _____

  _____

  _____

- List below the two rewards of right choices as revealed in this week's study:

  God's _____

  God's _____

- Have you ever enjoyed God's protection and provision as a result of choosing right? If so, describe it below.

_____

_____

_____

_____

- Have you ever told the young person(s) you love about the blessings you've enjoyed as a result of choosing right?
  ❏ Yes ❏ No

How can you do so more often? _____

_____

- Using Jeremiah 29:11 as a guide, spend a few moments in prayer, thanking God for the plans He has for you.

  "For I know the plans I have for you," declares the Lord, "plans to prosper you and not to harm you, plans to give you hope and a future."

WEEKLY JOURNAL

I learned that _____

_____

_____

One attitude I had which changed was _____

_____

_____

God spoke to me by _____

_____

_____

One behavior that I will examine is _____

_____

_____

When I shared with the child or youth in my life, _____

_____

_____

The most difficult thing was _____

_____

_____

It was a joy to _____

_____

_____

Tomorrow I will _____

_____

_____

My Scripture memory verse is_____

_____

The 4Cs

Who's the Boss? was the name of a popular American TV sit-com in the 80s. The plot of the show involved a single-mother professional who hired a single father as a housekeeper and baby-sitter. The title apparently referred to the fact that employer and employee frequently became confused over their roles. The woman was in charge, but they often struggled to keep their non-traditional roles and families straight.

Something similar goes on between God and His creation. It all started long before *Who's the Boss?*, of course, long before TV.

You'll discover more about "Who's the Boss?" in this week's study, and you'll also learn how you and others can keep from making the fundamental mistake of forgetting or denying "Who's the Boss?" Making the right choices in today's world is difficult. Our culture has told us that the model of truth which focuses on "me" and not on God is the way to make decisions. Such a warped view of truth and morality allows us to be selfish and to do what feels good instead of what God says is right.

Four simple steps, if learned by adults and taught to children and youth, will equip this generation to make right moral choices every time. This week's study explores that process called "The 4Cs."

This week you will—
- confront your tendency to resist the Truth and reject right choices;
- learn the four steps to making right moral choices; and
- discover how to begin teaching these to children and youth.

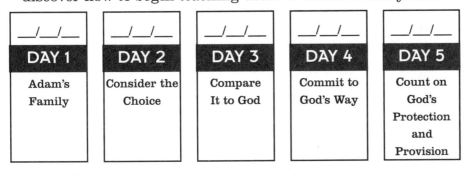

__/__/__	__/__/__	__/__/__	__/__/__	__/__/__
DAY 1	**DAY 2**	**DAY 3**	**DAY 4**	**DAY 5**
Adam's Family	Consider the Choice	Compare It to God	Commit to God's Way	Count on God's Protection and Provision

(Add the day/month/year to indicate when you complete your study.)

A key verse to memorize
   " 'For my thoughts are not your thoughts, neither are your ways my ways,' declares the Lord" (Isaiah 55:8).

Concepts you will come to understand

- The 4Cs:
    Consider the Choice
    Compare It to God
    Commit to God's Way
    Count on God's Protection and Provision

This Week's Assignments

- Memorize Isaiah 55:8.
- Complete your daily exercises.
- Make a conscious effort to approach (and later evaluate) your decisions this week using the 4Cs process. When you succeed, share with your significant child or teenager how the 4Cs process helped guide your judgment. If you fail, share with your young person what your mistake was and how you hope to follow the 4Cs process in making the right choice the next time.
- Take advantage of every opportunity to impress upon the children and youth in your life God's motivation to provide and protect. Use safety belts, fences, traffic laws, and rules and restrictions within your own life to illustrate how God issues His precepts, not to spoil our fun, but to protect and provide for us. Endeavor to help children and youth see the physical, emotional, psychological, and relational benefits that God wants us to enjoy.
- Complete your Weekly Journal.

Adam's Family

DAY ONE

The serpent snuck up behind the woman.

"Hey, Eve!" he said. "Why haven't you tried that fruit tree at the center of the garden?"

"God told me not to," Eve answered.

"God really said you couldn't eat from all these fruit trees?" The serpent would have swept an arm around to indicate the many fruit trees that surrounded them, but serpents don't have arms.

"No," she answered. "God just said we couldn't eat from *that* tree—couldn't even touch it, I think He said, or we would die."

"Aw, you're kidding me! You won't die from touching that ol' tree. God just doesn't want you going near it because He knows if you eat that fruit you'll become like Him."

Eve looked puzzled.

"Let me break it down for you. God is saying He's the only one who can define what is truly right and wrong. And, to make things worse, He's got the gall to try to impose it on you. That's not right, Eve. You have what it takes to determine for yourself what is good and evil. You don't have to accept God's ideas. You can figure that out yourself. You can have it your way. You have the power to define truth within yourself—just like God does. Now doesn't that sound good?"

The serpent's spiel worked, of course, and Eve ate the fruit. But not only had the serpent convinced her that she was capable of judging good and evil, as we discussed above; he had also persuaded her to believe that she didn't need God to define right and wrong, but that she could decide such things on her own: that she didn't need an outside, objective standard, but could be her *own* standard. She later enticed her husband, Adam, to eat. They were both kicked out of the garden, and went elsewhere to raise Adam's family.

The Serpent's Technique

Read Genesis 3:1-5 on the following page. In these verses, we discover that the serpent persuaded the woman to reject God's view of right and wrong. Circle the words in which the tempter planted doubt in the woman's mind about the reasonableness of God's command.

¹Now the serpent was more crafty than any of the wild animals the LORD God had made. He said to the woman, "Did God really say, 'You must not eat from any tree in the garden?' "

²The woman said to the serpent, "We may eat fruit from the trees in the garden, ³but God did say, 'You must not eat fruit from the tree that is in the middle of the garden, and you must not touch it, or you will die.' "

⁴"You will not surely die," the serpent said to the woman. ⁵"For God knows that when you eat of it your eyes will be opened, and you will be like God, knowing good and evil."

The serpent prompted the woman to doubt God. Underline the serpent's words that planted doubt in the woman's mind about God's truthfulness.

The serpent enticed the woman to doubt God's motivation. Bracket the serpent's words below that planted doubt in the woman's mind about God's motivation.

Read Genesis 3:6-10, 23 below.

⁶When the woman saw that the fruit of the tree was good for food and pleasing to the eye, and also desirable for gaining wisdom, she took some and ate it. She also gave some to her husband, who was with her, and he ate it. ⁷Then the eyes of both of them were opened, and they realized they were naked; so they sewed fig leaves together and made coverings for themselves.

⁸Then the man and his wife heard the sound of the LORD God as he was walking in the garden in the cool of the day, and they hid from the LORD God among the trees of the garden. ⁹But the LORD God called to the man, "Where are you?"

¹⁰He answered, "I heard you in the garden, and I was afraid because I was naked; so I hid."

²³So the LORD God banished him from the Garden of Eden to work the ground from which he had been taken.

According to these verses, what were the first results of Adam and Eve's rebellion? Check all that apply.
❑ They got food poisoning.
❑ They experienced guilt and shame for the first time.
❑ They invented applesauce.
❑ They were kicked out of the garden.
❑ They damaged their relationship with God.
❑ They lost their purity, innocence, and happiness.
❑ They decided never to trust a snake again.

Read Genesis 3:11-13 below.

> [11]And he said, "Who told you that you were naked? Have you eaten from the tree that I commanded you not to eat from?"
>
> [12]The man said, "The woman you put here with me—she gave me some fruit from the tree, and I ate it."
>
> [13]Then the LORD God said to the woman, "What is this you have done?"
>
> The woman said, "The serpent deceived me, and I ate."

The man and the woman had similar reactions when God asked them what they had done—they tried to blame someone else.

Whom did Adam try to blame?
- ❑ Eve
- ❑ God
- ❑ The serpent

Whom did Eve try to blame?
- ❑ God
- ❑ Adam
- ❑ The serpent

God's Way or My Way?

Not much has changed since Adam and Eve. The devil still tries to get us to doubt God's precepts, His person, and His motivation. We still suffer unhappy consequences from wrong choices. And we try to excuse our wrong choices by:
- blaming someone else;
- saying, "I didn't know it was wrong";
- claiming, "I had no choice";
- explaining that it really wasn't wrong in our case; or,
- justifying our actions because they weren't as bad as what other people have done.

None of these excuses really work. Ultimately our struggles about right and wrong come down to a struggle between our way and God's way. The real issue usually isn't, "What's right and what's wrong?" but "Whose version of right and wrong will I accept—mine or God's?"

Satan—in the guise of a serpent—convinced Eve that it wouldn't be so bad to reject God's version of right and wrong in favor of her own version. But we know how that turned out, don't we?

Decisions, Decisions

Some of us as parents, pastors, teachers, or children or youth leaders are flabbergasted that young people don't seem to know right from wrong these days. Yet, if we're totally honest, we would probably have to admit that our choices reveal that we often choose our way over God's way. If the truth be told, we often (by our actions, if not by our words) reject God's version of right and wrong in favor of our own customized version.

Before we can communicate truth to the next generation, we must confront our own tendencies to resist the Truth and reject right choices.

• Are you willing to admit that God is the *only* righteous judge, and that He alone can decide right and wrong? ❑ Yes ❑ No

• Are you ready to submit to God's version of right and wrong and follow what He says as right? ❑ Yes ❑ No

If your answer to both questions is *yes*, you're ready to take the following steps of submission.

1. *Turn from your selfish ways (repent and confess your sin) and admit that God is God.* "If we confess our sins, he is faithful and just and will forgive us our sins and purify us from all unrighteousness" (1 John 1:9). Acknowledge that you have been living contrary to God's ways, that you have been trying to go your own way. Agree that your own way is wrong, and that only God defines what is right and wrong.

2. *Submit to God as Savior and Lord. Commit to His ways.* If God can keep planets spinning in space, rivers running to the seas, and seasons coming and going, do you think He will mess up your life if you give him control? Hand your life over to Him, and depend on Him for the power to make right choices. A simple, heartfelt prayer such as the following can open your soul to the love and light of God.

> *Lord Jesus, I want to know You personally, the One who knows my future and has my best interests at heart. Thank You for dying on the cross for my sins and rising from the dead on the third day. Forgive me of my sins. I open the door of my life and trust You as my Savior and Lord. Thank You for forgiving my sins and giving me eternal life. Take control of my life. By the power of Your Holy Spirit, make me the kind of person You want me to be, and help me make the kind of choices You want me to make, amen.*

If you have already trusted Christ for salvation, but you've been rejecting God's authority and trying to decide right and wrong on your own, pray the following.

> *Father God, I need You. I acknowledge that I have been directing my life and that, as a result, I have sinned against You. I thank You that You have forgiven my sins through Christ's death on the cross for me. I now invite Christ again to take His place on the throne of my life. By the power of Your Holy Spirit, enable me to commit to Your ways and make right moral choices. In Jesus' name, amen.*

Trusting God to fill you with His Spirit doesn't mean that you will never again lack faith or be disobedient. But you can live more consistently if you daily admit God's sovereignty, sincerely submit to His loving authority, and employ a simple process every time you face a moral choice. It's that process we will be discussing throughout this week.

Close today's study time in prayer, admitting God's sovereignty and submitting to His authority. Ask God to guide you and speak to you the rest of this week through His Word.

DAY TWO

Consider the Choice

When my children were very young, I watched them navigate a maze at a small amusement park. The maze was sunk into a pit, so that from my vantage point above the pit, I was able to watch the children thread through it. Their confused meanderings seemed so pointless as they pursued one dead end after another. *Of course,* I reflected, *anyone can see the way to go from up here.*

From His vantage point, God can see the way through the moral maze so much better than we; and His commands are given to keep us from heading down dead ends (*Right From Wrong,* 106).

A maze is like life in so many ways. It's filled with decisions and dead ends. A maze can be frustrating, and it can be rewarding.

Most of us navigate the moral maze of life with less care and forethought than we give to the crossword puzzle in the Sunday paper. Most of us complete a maze in a puzzle book by pausing to think ahead every time we're faced with a choice between two directions. But we don't often do that in life.

• An opportunity arises to hide some income from the IRS, and we don't give it a thought. We just do it.

• We hear some juicy news about the pastor of a church across town, and we don't hesitate to repeat it. We just do it.

• We're flattered and excited by the flirtatious attentions of a coworker, and we don't stop to think about whether we should encourage such behavior. We just do it.

Every one of those "little" choices, like the frequent forks in a child's maze, represents a choice between the right path and the wrong path. Every decision represents an opportunity to select God's way or our way. That's why the first step in submitting to God is to consider the choice. To consider the choice means to stop and ask, "Who determines what is right or wrong in this situation?" It means to remind yourself that your choice is not between what you think is right and what you think is wrong; it's between what is objectively right and what is objectively wrong, regardless of what you think.

Write in the margin the Scripture memory verse, Isaiah 55:8. Say it aloud five times. Meditate on these words. Pray, asking God to help you take these words to heart.

Joseph's Choice

Read Genesis 39:1-10, the story of Joseph and Potiphar's wife.

> [1]Now Joseph had been taken down to Egypt. Potiphar, an Egyptian who was one of Pharaoh's officials, the captain of the guard, bought him from the Ishmaelites who had taken him there.
> [2]The LORD was with Joseph and he prospered, and he lived in the house of his Egyptian master. [3]When his master saw that the Lord was with him and that the Lord gave him success in everything he did, [4]Joseph found favor in his eyes and became his attendant. Potiphar put him in charge of his household, and he entrusted to his care everything he owned. [5]From the time he put him in charge of his household and of all that he owned, the Lord blessed the household of the Egyptian because of Joseph. The blessing of the Lord was on everything Potiphar had, both in the house and in the field. [6]So he left in Joseph's care everything he had; with Joseph in charge, he did not concern himself with anything except the food he ate.
> Now Joseph was well-built and handsome, [7]and after a while his master's wife took notice of Joseph and said, "Come to bed with me!"
> [8]But he refused. "With me in charge," he told her, "my master does not concern himself with anything in the house; everything he owns he has entrusted to my care. [9]No one is greater in this house than I am. My master has withheld nothing from me except you, because you are his wife. How then could I do such a wicked thing and sin against God?" [10]And though she spoke to Joseph day after day, he refused to go to bed with her or even be with her.

Change the following statements to make them correct. Mark out the incorrect words or phrases and write the correct ones in their place.

1. God blessed Andujar's household because of Joseph (v. 5).

2. Potiphar's wife noticed Joseph because he took steroids (vv. 6-7).

3. Joseph responded to his master's wife without thinking (vv. 7-9).

4. Joseph accepted the advances of Potiphar's wife because, he said, "no one is greater in this house than I am" (vv. 8-9).

5. Joseph had trouble seeing which choice would be right and which would be wrong (vv. 8-9).

6. Joseph had to face this temptation and make this choice once (v. 10).

Do you think …
❑ Joseph considered his choice carefully?
❑ Joseph just made a decision suddenly, without any deliberation?

What part of the passage supports your answer? _____

_____

_____

Reviewing Today's Study

The first step in submitting to God is: C _____

When you are faced with a moral choice, do you see it as a choice between going … your way?   ❑ yes
                                                ❑ no
                                                ❑ sometimes

                          … God's way?   ❑ yes
                                           ❑ no
                                           ❑ sometimes

Do you … ❑ tend to consider the choice carefully, or
         ❑ make a decision suddenly, without thinking?

What can you do in the future to consider the choice between your way and God's way?

_____

_____

_____

Look at Psalm 25:4-5 below. Pray those words to God several times, making them truly the prayer of your heart.

Show me your ways, O Lord, teach me your paths; guide me in your truth and teach me, for you are God my Savior, and my hope is in you all day long.

Compare It to God

Too often, parents and other adults communicate to young people that their actions violate the *adult's* standard of decency, or ethics, or morality. That would be perfectly appropriate if absolute truth were defined by the individual. But it's not. It is God and God alone who determines absolute truth. ...we must be certain our young people understand that right and wrong are not measured by our own standards, but by the nature and character of God (*Right From Wrong*, 82-83).

So you've *admitted* God's authority, and sincerely *submitted* to Him and His "version" (the only true version) of right and wrong. You've even begun to consider your choices a lot more than ever before. In the moment of decision you're learning to see simple everyday choices as choices between what is objectively right and what is objectively wrong.

You've made the first step in daily submitting your will to God and following His ways. The next step—after considering the choice—is to compare it to God.

In other words, after you weigh the choice you're facing in any situation, and acknowledge that it presents the opportunity to choose rightly or wrongly, you can proceed to compare your choice of action to the person of God. For example:

• When you flip through the cable channels and discover a steamy sex scene, you (1) consider the choice, recognizing it as an opportunity for a right or wrong decision, and (2) compare it to God.

• When your insurance adjustor asks if the dent on the front fender you know was from a previous incident is part of your recent car accident, you (1) consider the choice, recognizing it as an opportunity for a right or wrong decision, and (2) compare it to God.

• When a waitress incorrectly totals your lunch tab, saving you just enough cash to buy your spouse a card on the way home, you (1) consider the choice, recognizing it as an opportunity for a right or wrong decision, and (2) compare it to God.

How do you compare it to God? By using the truth process you learned last week. Write the three key words that express that process on the next page.

P _____

P _____

P _____

Joseph's Standard

Read Genesis 39:1-10 from yesterday's study (p. 75). Answer the questions that follow.

What godly principles would Joseph have violated if he had given in to Potiphar's wife?

_____

_____

_____

In what ways was Joseph's behavior—toward Potiphar, toward Potiphar's wife, toward God Himself—like the person of God?

_____

_____

_____

What part of the scriptural account indicates that Joseph did, in fact, compare his action to the person of God? Underline those verses.

Although Joseph lived centuries before the Ten Commandments were given to the nation of Israel, his attitudes and actions reveal a strong knowledge of the precepts, principles, and person of God.

Which of the Ten Commandments (precepts) would have applied to Joseph's situation? Check it in the following list from Exodus 20.

❏ v. 3—You shall have no other gods before me.

❏ v. 4—You shall not make for yourself an idol in the form of anything in heaven above or on the earth beneath or in the waters below.

❏ v. 7—You shall not misuse the name of the LORD your God.

❏ v. 8—Remember the Sabbath day by keeping it holy.

❏ v. 12—Honor your father and your mother.

❏ v. 13—You shall not murder.

❏ v. 14—You shall not commit adultery.

❏ v. 15—You shall not steal.

❏ v. 16—You shall not give false testimony against your neighbor.

❏ v. 17—You shall not covet.

Reviewing Today's Study

The first two steps of submission to God are:

C_____

C_____

Seems rather simple, doesn't it? It's not that difficult to remember. Of course, living a life that reflects submission to God is another matter.

Are you facing any choices right now to which you can apply these first two steps? ❏ Yes ❏ No

If you answered yes, complete the following statements.

If I look at this particular situation as an opportunity for doing what is objectively right or wrong, I would

_____

_____

If I compare this particular action to the person of God, I would

_____

Complete at least two of the following statements.

I'm thinking: _____

_____

_____

I'm feeling: _____

_____

_____

I'm bothered about: _____

_____

_____

I'm excited about: _____

_____

I want to pray about: _____

_____

Spend a few moments in prayer using the following as a guide.
- Talk to God honestly about the statements you've made above.
- Ask God to give you patience and perseverance as you continue this study.
- Pray for the needs and concerns of the young people in your life.

Commit to God's Way

Your plane has just landed in a strange city. You flag a cab outside the airport, wrestle your luggage in ahead of you, and climb into the musky confines of the back seat. The cab driver, who speaks English as well as you speak Urdu, asks where you want to go. You give him the address of your hotel, and you're on your way.

You lean back in the cab, casting furtive glances at the cabbie's license and at the newspapers and food wrappers that litter the seat and floor (hoping to locate the rotting animal carcass that's causing the cab to smell the way it does).

Finally, when it seems as if you've been in the cab for four or five days, you notice that the scenery seems to be repeating itself. That burned-out car frame outside your window looks familiar, and the woman picking through the trash cans just looked up and waved at you like an old friend. You lean forward and, speaking slowly and clearly, ask the driver if it will be much farther to the hotel.

The driver turns around and faces you without slowing down. He answers you excitedly, but the only words you recognize are "hotel" and "terrible."

"Are we lost?" you ask.

"No, no, no, no, no, no," the driver says, before launching into another string of unintelligible words.

"Should you ask directions?" you suggest, reasoning that he must understand English better than he speaks it.

"No," the man answers. "I know where to go."

The words are barely out of his mouth before he turns past a sign that reads, "No outlet." He slams the brakes at the end of the street, shoves the gear lever into park, and picks up the radio microphone. He prattles foreign words rapidly into the device, then, like an ocean breeze on a hot summer day, you hear a voice over the radio, a voice speaking in clear English.

"Ah, you wanna turn around, go back to Burnet Avenue," the radio voice answers, the popping sound of chewing gum accompanying the directions. "Right at the light, two miles, hang a left at the bottling company. Another left, and you're in the hotel parking lot."

"But you turned left back there," you say. Another shrug. Another cryptic comment.

"You're going the wrong way," you say.

"No, no, no," the driver answers, speaking loudly, as if your problem is hearing, not understanding. "I get there. I go my way."

You slump back in your seat. You gaze out the window, wondering if there are cab drivers in the Bermuda Triangle.

That's rather unrealistic, isn't it? No one would get directions from someone who knows the way and then choose to ignore them.

But we do that all the time. So do today's children and youth. God has given us directions in the form of precepts that point to principles that spring from His person. Yet we often choose to go our own way rather than follow directions from God, the One who knows the way.

For that reason, even when we consider the choice and compare it to God, we still must commit to His way. Once we have compared our selfish desires to God's absolute standard, we must choose between our way and God's way. We must consciously turn from our selfish ways and resolutely commit to God's way.

You breathe a sigh of relief; there is hope, after all. Your driver mutters a few syllables, turns the cab around, drives to the end of the street, and turns left at the next light.

"Excuse me," you say, leaning forward again. "The man on the radio said to turn right at the light." The man shrugs and chatters a response.

Joseph's Determination

Read Genesis 39:1-10 on page 75. Then read verses 11-12 below. Respond to the statements that follow by circling *T* (True) or *F* (False).

> [11]One day he went into the house to attend to his duties, and none of the household servants was inside. [12]She caught him by his cloak and said, "Come to bed with me!" But he left his cloak in her hand and ran out of the house.

T F Joseph had to face the temptation posed by Potiphar's wife many times.

T F Joseph didn't think what she had in mind was wrong; he just didn't find her attractive.

T F Joseph refused to go to bed with Potiphar's wife, but he still followed her.

T F Joseph's behavior shows that he was committed to obeying God.

T F Joseph committed to God's way because it was convenient.

T F Committing to God's way apparently meant to Joseph that he would try to do the right thing.

Joseph did the right thing in the face of unremitting temptation because he ...

- <u>considered</u> the choice (recognizing that his situation involved a choice between what was objectively right and what was objectively wrong, regardless of his situation),
- <u>compared</u> it to God (recognizing that sexual involvement with Potiphar's wife would have contradicted the nature and character of a God who is pure, faithful, and trustworthy), and
- <u>committed</u> to God's way, (deciding that he would accept God's "directions" and adjust his behavior accordingly). Verse ten makes it clear that Joseph planned his behavior to help him commit daily to God's way.

Write in the margin the Scripture memory verse, Isaiah 55:8. Say it aloud once before continuing today's study.

Your Way, God's Way

Are you ready to commit to God's way? It's the kind of commitment you make every time you're faced with a moral choice. It means turning from your selfish ways and saying, "God, I see that Your way is right, and I commit to following You, with Your help, in the power of Your Holy Spirit."

Are you ready to put your commitment in writing, a kind of "manifesto," to guide you in your future decision-making? Following is an example of such a commitment:

"I will *consider* my choices carefully. I will *compare* my attitudes and actions to God and His Word I will turn from my selfishness that causes me to look for excuses to justify my behavior and *commit* to God's ways. I will allow God's Holy Spirit to empower me to make right moral choices."

Use the lines below to record your own prayer to God—your own "manifesto" for making right moral choices.

_____

_____

_____

_____

In tomorrow's study you will discover the final step in the 4Cs process. Remember as you study and learn that, while you may be studying this material in order to address the crisis of truth among the young people you love, this process needs to be practiced and displayed in your life before it can be effectively imparted to others.

Reviewing Today's Study

The first two steps of submission to God are:

C_____

C_____

C_____

You may be discovering that your own moral decision-making has lacked one or more of the elements. If that's the case, take a few moments to confess to God that deficiency and any effects it has had on your life and on the lives of your family and friends. Surrender to God, and ask for His healing and restoration in specific areas.

Seal your commitment with a prayer to God, telling Him your determination when faced with a moral choice, to:
• Consider the choice;
• Compare it to God;
• Commit to God's way.

Count on God's Protection and Provision

Once you have considered the choice, compared it to God, and then committed to God's way, there is one final step in the process of submitting to the Sovereign Lord: count on God's protection and provision.

When we humbly admit God's sovereignty and sincerely submit to His loving authority, we will not only begin to see clearly the distinctions between right and wrong, but we will also begin to count on God's protection and provision.

This doesn't mean that everything will be rosy; in fact, God says rather bluntly that you may sometimes suffer for righteousness' sake (see Matthew 5:10-11). Even such suffering has rewards. Living according to God's way and allowing the Holy Spirit to live through you brings many spiritual blessings. Some blessings include freedom from guilt, a clear conscience, the joy of sharing Christ, and (most importantly) the blessing of God upon your life.

You can also enjoy many physical, emotional, psychological, and relational benefits when you commit to God's ways. While God's protection and provision should not be the primary motivation for obeying God, it certainly provides a powerful encouragement for choosing right and rejecting wrong!

An ancient newspaper account (discovered by archaeologists from Central Bogus University) will help reveal the experience of one person who considered the choice, compared it to God, committed to God's ways, and counted on God's protection and provision.

High Official Disgraced

MEMPHIS, EGYPT—Joseph ben Jacob, a civil servant in the Hyksos administration, was arrested this morning on charges that he assaulted the wife of an unnamed superior. Potiphar, the captain of the guard and investigating officer in the case, confirmed the report.

The wife, despite the trauma caused by her experience, initially reported the incident to her household servants. When her husband arrived home, she told him and presented evidence of the assault, a cloak her attacker left behind as he fled.

Joseph is being held without bail in the king's prison in Memphis. No trial date has been set.

Authorities Won't Reveal Victim's Identity

MEMPHIS, EGYPT—Government officials refused to release the name of the woman who accused Joseph ben Jacob of assault Tuesday, saying only that she is the trusted wife of an influential official.

Some highly placed sources report that the Queen and her entourage were away from the capital on a pleasure cruise down the Nile at the reported time of the incident, so the queen is certainly not the victim.

Rumors in the halls of government place the wife of Potiphar, the captain of the guard, at the center of the story. She has so far refused to talk with reporters.

Accused Has Checkered Past

MEMPHIS, EGYPT—The non-Egyptian who yesterday was accused of assaulting a government official's wife allegedly has a record of violent encounters in the past.

Unnamed sources are quoted as saying that Joseph ben Jacob arrived in Egypt some years ago after narrowly escaping death in a family quarrel. After his own brothers imprisoned him (an act of mercy to avert execution for previous crimes), he was delivered from captivity by Potiphar, the arresting officer in this sordid case.

Joseph's own father is an acknowledged perjurer and extortionist, known to have built his ranching empire by stealing from his brother and father-in-law.

The family of the accused was last known to be living in tents and roaming the land of Canaan with their flocks of sheep.

Accused Maintains Innocence

MEMPHIS, EGYPT—Joseph ben Jacob, who lost his position yesterday as a trusted civil servant due to charges of assault, has steadfastly maintained his innocence, saying, "How could I do such a wicked thing and sin against God?"

Potiphar, who has not appointed an attorney to defend the accused, responded to reports of Joseph's statement by saying, "It's the word of a Hebrew servant against that of a government official's wife. Who would you believe?"

Compare the newspaper accounts to Genesis 39:13-20 below and on the following page.

¹³When she saw that he had left his cloak in her hand and had run out of the house, ¹⁴she called her household servants. "Look," she said to them, "this Hebrew has been brought to us to make sport of us! He came in here to sleep with me, but I screamed. ¹⁵When he heard me scream for help, he left his cloak beside me and ran out of the house."

¹⁶She kept his cloak beside her until his master came home. ¹⁷Then she told him this story: "That Hebrew slave you brought us came to me to make sport of me. But as soon as I screamed for help, he left his cloak beside me and ran out of the house."

¹⁹When his master heard the story his wife told him, saying, "This is how your slave treated me," he burned with anger. ²⁰Joseph's master took him and put him in prison, the place where the king's prisoners were confined.

1. What were the immediate results of Joseph's choice? Check all that apply.
   ❏ He was disgraced and imprisoned.
   ❏ He earned a guest appearance on four talk shows.
   ❏ He was falsely accused of wrongdoing.
   ❏ He lost the trust of his boss.
   ❏ He accepted a position with a powerful government lobbying firm.

2. Do these accounts make it seem like Joseph enjoyed rewards for choosing to do right? ❏ Yes ❏ No

3. Do you think the consequences of Joseph's actions made him sorry he had committed to God's way? ❏ Yes ❏ No
   Why or why not?

   _____

   _____

   _____

Joseph's Reward

"Oh great," you may say. "What an endorsement for submitting all my decisions to God! I can hear my kids now: 'Commit to God's way, get falsely accused of a terrible crime, go to prison—where do I sign up?'"

That's not the end of the story. Remember, doing the right thing may not bring immediate rewards. But did Joseph suffer in the long run for committing to God's ways and following His directions? Let's see.

Read Genesis 39:21-23 below and on the following page. What was Joseph's experience in prison? Briefly outline the chain of events on the following page.

²¹But while Joseph was there in the prison, the LORD was with him; he showed him kindness and granted him favor in the eyes of the prison warden. ²²So the warden put Joseph in charge of all those held in the prison, and he was made responsible for all that was done there. ²³The warden paid no attention to anything under Joseph's care, because the LORD was with Joseph and gave him success in whatever he did.

_____

_____

_____

_____

Do you think the integrity he displayed in his former position helped him earn the prison warden's confidence? ❏ Yes ❏ No Why or why not?

_____

_____

Read Genesis 41:38-52.

38So Pharaoh asked them, "Can we find anyone like this man, one in whom is the spirit of God?"

39Then Pharaoh said to Joseph, "Since God has made all this known to you, there is no one so discerning and wise as you. 40You shall be in charge of my palace, and all my people are to submit to your orders. Only with respect to the throne will I be greater than you."

41So Pharaoh said to Joseph, "I hereby put you in charge of the whole land of Egypt." 42Then Pharaoh took his signet ring from his finger and put it on Joseph's finger. He dressed him in robes of fine linen and put a gold chain around his neck. 43He had him ride in a chariot as his second-in-command, and men shouted before him, "Make way!" Thus he put him in charge of the whole land of Egypt.

44Then Pharaoh said to Joseph, "I am Pharaoh, but without your word no one will lift hand or foot in all Egypt." 45Pharaoh gave Joseph the name Zaphenath-Paneah and gave him Asenath daughter of Potiphera, priest of On, to be his wife. And Joseph went throughout the land of Egypt.

46Joseph was thirty years old when he entered the service of Pharaoh king of Egypt. And Joseph went out from Pharaoh's presence and traveled throughout Egypt. 47During the seven years of abundance the land produced plentifully. 48Joseph collected all the food produced in those seven years of abundance in Egypt and stored it in the cities. In each city he put the food grown in the fields surrounding it. 49Joseph stored up huge quantities of grain, like the sand of the sea; it was so much that he stopped keeping records because it was beyond measure.

⁵⁰Before the years of famine came, two sons were born to Joseph by Asenath daughter of Potiphera, priest of On. ⁵¹Joseph named his firstborn Manasseh and said, "It is because God has made me forget all my trouble and all my father's household." ⁵²The second son he named Ephraim and said, "It is because God has made me fruitful in the land of my suffering."

What benefits did Joseph eventually enjoy as a result of God's protection and provision? Check all that apply.

❑ wisdom
❑ integrity
❑ a new car
❑ a good reputation
❑ a gold watch
❑ authority
❑ the favor of God

❑ free cable
❑ power
❑ wealth
❑ a wife and children
❑ paid holidays
❑ a clear conscience
❑ popularity

Responding to the 4Cs

There you have it … the 4Cs for submitting every moral choice to the Sovereign Lord who knows you, the future, and what's best.

Let's review the 4Cs process we have learned this week. Close your eyes and see if you can repeat in your mind and then out loud each step. Then check and see how well you remembered these steps.

The 4Cs Process

1. Consider the Choice.
   Ask, "Who determines what is right or wrong in this situation?"

2. Compare It to God.
   Admit that God is God and compare your attitude and action to His Word (which reflects His character and nature).

3. Commit to God's Way.
   Turn from your selfish ways and submit to God's sovereign Lordship.

4. Count on God's Protection and Provision.
   Thank God for His loving motivation to provide for and protect us.

As you continue in this study, you will use the 4Cs process over and over again. Right now, however, give some thought to your commitment to the process.

Read Psalm 37:3-6 below.

> ³Trust in the Lord and do good; dwell in the land and enjoy safe pasture.
> ⁴Delight yourself in the Lord and he will give you the desires of your heart.
> ⁵Commit your way to the Lord; trust in him and he will do this:
> ⁶He will make your righteousness shine like the dawn, the justice of your cause like the noonday sun.

Verses 3, 4, and 5 begin with similar phrases. Circle those key phrases.

What kind of protection and provision will follow the kind of commitment the psalmist writes about? Write verses 4 and 6 below.

He will _____

_____
(v. 4).

He will _____

_____
(v. 6).

Are you ready to implement fully the 4Cs process in your life? ❏ Yes ❏ No   If the answer is yes, you are ready to challenge the children and youth in your life to do the same.

Reviewing Today's Study

The steps in the 4Cs process are:

C_____

C_____

C_____

C_____

Do you have trouble with any of the 4Cs? ❏ Yes ❏ No
If so, circle it in the list above.

What will you do to overcome the trouble you are experiencing?

_____

_____

_____

Read Psalm 37:3-6 again (p. 90) and close today's study in prayer. Change the words in the verses to reflect your commitment and trust. For example, you might pray, "I trust in You, Lord. I want to do good ... and I trust You to make my righteousness shine like the dawn."

WEEKLY JOURNAL

I learned that _____

_____

_____

One attitude I had which changed was _____

_____

_____

God spoke to me by _____

_____

_____

One behavior that I will examine is _____

_____

_____

When I shared with the child or youth in my life, _____

_____

_____

The most difficult thing was _____

_____

_____

It was a joy to _____

_____

_____

Tomorrow I will _____

_____

_____

My Scripture memory verse is _____

_____

The Honest Truth

WEEK FOUR

"Man, I never would have believed it if I hadn't seen it!"

Two doctors stood in the hospital hallway. One just emerged from the delivery room; he removed a green mask from his face. The other stopped to listen to his friend's story.

"What wouldn't you believe?" the second doctor asked.

"The baby I just delivered. I've never seen anything like it!"

"Like what?"

"Well," the first doctor said, "I pulled the little guy out, you know, no problem."

"Yeah?"

"Cut the umbilical cord."

"Yeah," the other said, impatience creeping into his voice.

"And then I handed the kid to his father, who set the little tyke down on the floor."

"He laid a newborn baby on the floor?"

"I didn't say he laid him down. He just set him down ... on his feet. And the kid stood there for a few seconds."

"A newborn baby stood up by himself?" The second doctor shook his head and then looked suspiciously at his friend. "You're pulling my leg."

"No, I'm serious! He stood right there on that delivery room floor, just like he'd been doing it all his life. Well, come to think of it, he had been doing it all of his born life."

"Then what happened?"

"You won't believe it. He picked a cotton ball off the floor, tossed it in the air and caught it a couple times, and then made a mad dash for the trash can."

"He ran? You must think I'm some kind of fool."

"No, no, it's true. And when he got to the trash can—which was about four times his height—he leaped, twisted his body in the air, extended his arms, and dunked that little piece of cotton like it was a basketball."

"Yeah, yeah. Real funny." The second doctor started to walk away.

"I'm not playing around!" the first doctor shouted after his departing friend. "I saw it with my own two eyes. This Michael Jordan kid is incredible!"

That story is ridiculous, of course. Michael Jordan may be among the greatest athletes of all time, but he still had to learn to stand, walk, and run as a child. He even had to learn how to play basketball, just like everyone else. By the time he retired from basketball to pursue a baseball career, Jordan had set all kinds of records and helped his team win three straight national championships. And then he returned to basketball to add to those records!

It's amazing what practice can do. It can make a difficult game look easy. Practice can make a complex skill seem effortless. It can make a process of several steps feel natural.

That's what this week's study is all about. You'll practice applying the 4Cs to a real-life situation in which you must decide which action would be right, which would be wrong, and how you would communicate that to the significant young person in your life. That process can be even more difficult than sinking a half-court shot with one second left in the game.

This week you will—
• learn God's truth about honesty;
• discover how to apply honesty to real-life situations;
• unmask justifications we make to cover our dishonest attitudes and actions; and
• explore how to teach honesty to children and youth.

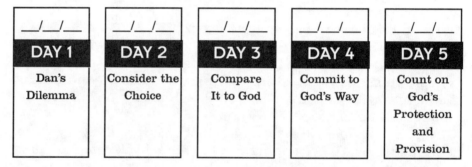

__/__/__	__/__/__	__/__/__	__/__/__	__/__/__
DAY 1	**DAY 2**	**DAY 3**	**DAY 4**	**DAY 5**
Dan's Dilemma	Consider the Choice	Compare It to God	Commit to God's Way	Count on God's Protection and Provision

(Add the day/month/year to indicate when you complete your study.)

A key verse to memorize
    "I know, my God, that you test the heart and are pleased with integrity" (1 Chronicles 29:17).

Concepts you will come to understand
• Honesty is rooted in the nature of God who is True.
• The long-term benefits of God's protection and provision outweigh the short-term pleasure of dishonesty.
• Honesty is reflected in a relationship with a young person.

This Week's Assignments

- Memorize 1 Chronicles 29:17.
- Complete daily exercises.
- Play the "what if" game. Ask your young person to imagine how the world would be different if everyone were absolutely honest. Some answers might include: we wouldn't have to lock doors, chain things down, install alarm systems, pay theft insurance. Lead a discussion of how honesty protects and provides for us.
- Role play with your children and youth some of the following situations forcing a choice about honesty.
  (1) You can win the game, but only if you cheat.
  (2) You know your friend is lying to the teacher about where he was at lunch.
  (3) You see something you really want but can't have unless you steal it.
- For teenagers, discuss a news item or current event at school, work, or in the community that illustrates the consequences of dishonesty and the benefits of honesty. With a younger child, try to "catch" him or her being honest so you can reward honesty. This behavior need not be heroic; simply returning change to Mom or Dad after a purchase or admitting that a chore has been neglected is sufficient. Express appreciation and congratulations—perhaps with an extended curfew or a bonus added to an allowance to say, "I noticed (and I value) your honesty."
- Complete your Weekly Journal.

DAY ONE

Dan's Dilemma

Dan barely made it to his chemistry exam. His mom had been in the hospital for four days now, and he'd been spending every waking moment at her bedside. He hadn't even heard the alarm go off this morning; by the time he awoke, it was 7:23 a.m. His chemistry final started at 8:05.

He slipped into his seat just as the tardy bell rang and breathed a weary sigh.

Ever since Mom's been sick, he thought, *I haven't been able to study like I should.*

He'd carried all As and Bs until the most recent grading period, but his grades had deteriorated since his mother had been hospitalized with cancer. He just didn't have the energy, it seemed, to study *and* take care of his mom.

So far he'd passed all his classes at least. But Mr. Henderson, his chemistry teacher, had this rule. You could get straight As all year, but if you flunked the last semester, you flunked the course. Dan had gotten Bs from Mr. Henderson so far, but he knew he wasn't ready for this final.

As he started the four-page final, Dan shook his head, trying to clear the cobwebs that seemed to hide the answers.

I know this stuff, he told himself. *I know I do. I just can't think straight these days.*

He trudged through page after page, alternately hopeful and despairing of his chances at passing the test—and the course.

He was beginning page three when Stephanie Andrews dropped a page from her test. It floated into the aisle and landed on the floor beside his chair. He glanced at Stephanie; she seemed not to notice, but something in the movement of her head suggested that the dropped page had not been an accident.

Stephanie had been a good friend to Dan. She had even visited his mom in the hospital. He looked from Stephanie to the others in the room. No one seemed to be paying any attention. Mr. Henderson sat at his desk in the corner of the room, only occasionally looking up from the papers he was grading.

Dan's eyes settled on Stephanie's neat handwriting. He could read the answers without difficulty. Dan's gaze returned to his own desk. He stared at the blank spaces on his test paper.

He began jotting the answers rapidly onto his own test. It was his only chance at passing the test—and the course, he figured. And it was only one page.

I knew those answers anyway, he told himself as he picked the page off the floor and handed it back to a sweetly smiling Stephanie. *I was just having trouble remembering them because of all that stuff with Mom. It's not like I'm cheating or anything. Not with everything I've had to worry about this month.*

You Make the Call

Have you ever found yourself as an adult in a similar situation—maybe as you took an exam for a promotion at work, as you tested for a real estate license, or when you applied for a driver's license?

What would you do—realistically—in a similar situation? What would you have done in your high school days? How would you advise a young person to handle a similar situation?

Keep in mind that there seem to be good, compelling reasons for making one choice or the other, especially to the mind of a young person. List those reasons below.

Reasons to use the answers Dan read on Stephanie's paper:

_____

Reasons not to use the answers Dan read on Stephanie's paper:

_____

What is motivating Dan in this situation? Check any that apply.
- ❑ a concern for his grades
- ❑ convenience
- ❑ his own selfish interests
- ❑ worry for his mother
- ❑ a desire to do the right thing
- ❑ thought for his college plans
- ❑ consideration for Stephanie's feelings
- ❑ a desire to make his mom proud of him
- ❑ an unwillingness to hurt Stephanie's feelings

Believe it or not, Dan's situation and his reasoning are quite common among our youth. The survey in the book *Right From Wrong* reveals that the majority of the youth in our churches and youth groups struggle with the moral issues confronting Dan.

> The research indicates that one of the areas in which our youth struggle most is the area of honesty. Two of every three (66 percent) say they have lied to a "parent, teacher, or other older person" within the last three months. Slightly fewer—six in ten (59 percent)—say they have lied to a friend or peer within the last three months. More than one-third (36 percent) admit that they have cheated on an exam or other evaluation within that same three month period, and nearly one-sixth (15 percent) say they have recently stolen money or other possessions (*Right From Wrong*, 169).

A Look at the Book

Of course, there's no Bible verse that says, "Dan shalt not copy from Stephanie's paper." There's no verse that says, "Dan *shall* copy from Stephanie's paper," either.

So how is Dan supposed to decide, then, which choice is right? How would you guide a young person in Dan's situation?

If you have a study Bible, use the concordance or topical index to help you answer the following questions.

What Bible verses might apply to Dan's situation? _____

_____

Probably one of the first verses to come to mind was Exodus 20:15, "You shall not steal." If you did not think of others, read below Leviticus 19:11; and 1 Corinthians 6:10.

> Do not steal. Do not lie. Do not deceive one another (Leviticus 19:11).

> ... nor thieves nor the greedy nor drunkards nor slanderers nor swindlers will inherit the kingdom of God (1 Corinthians 6:10).

What biblical concepts or principles apply to these verses?

_____

_____

Did you include honesty in your list?

As you continue this week's study, be honest and realistic about what choices you would make yourself under similar circumstances and why. You probably don't have a chemistry exam this week. But you face other situations similar to Dan's. Do you find yourself justifying any of the following situations? Check all that apply.
- ❑ "creative accounting" on income tax returns
- ❑ over-billing for goods or services
- ❑ padding an expense account
- ❑ taking credit for something you didn't do
- ❑ leaving work early without permission
- ❑ using business vehicles or equipment for unauthorized personal uses
- ❑ other _____

Would you interpret any of the above situations as being different from Dan's? ❑ Yes ❑ No If so, how? Be careful not to rationalize yourself out of an honest response.

_____

_____

Also as you continue this week's study, consider specific ways you can influence the decision-making processes of the significant children and youth in your life. If you were aware of Dan's situation, what could you do as a parent, teacher, youth minister, or adult friend?

Conclude today's study by reading 1 Chronicles 29:10-13; use those verses to guide you in a personal time of praise and adoration.

> David praised the LORD in the presence of the whole assembly saying,
> "Praise be to you, O LORD, God of our father Israel, from everlasting to everlasting.
> Yours, O LORD, is the greatness and the power and the glory and the majesty and the splendor, for everything in heaven and earth is yours.
> Yours, O LORD, is the kingdom; you are exalted as head over all.
> Wealth and honor come from you; you are the ruler of all things. In you hands are strength and power to exalt and give strength to all.
> Now, our God, we give you thanks, and praise your glorious name."

Conclude your prayer time by memorizing and meditating on 1 Chronicles 29:17:

> I know, my God, that you test the heart and are pleased with integrity.

DAY TWO

Consider the Choice

Dan, of course, is making a split-second decision. He doesn't have time to check his Bible and read through a workbook. That's how life is. Decisions about right or wrong are most often the result of a moment's thought or a split-second impulse.

Still, an amazing number of thoughts and impulses take place in that short amount of time. Through the miracle of modern science, we can take a peek into Dan's head and see the high-speed processes that took place just before his decision to copy the answers from Stephanie's paper.

❑ Self-pity—Ever since Mom's been sick, I haven't had time to study.
❑ Fear—If I fail the test, I'll fail the course.
❑ Worry—What if I get caught?
❑ Gratitude—Stephanie knows what I'm going through.
❑ Despair—I can't remember the answers!
❑ Weariness—Just do the easiest thing.
❑ Justification—I knew these answers anyway.
❑ Conscience—It's not right.
❑ Selfishness—What's in it for me?

If the human mind can process that amount of information in seconds, it can handle the 4Cs process. In fact, the 4Cs process can actually streamline decision-making, because it sorts all the various thoughts that assail the mind in a moment of decision.

So let's apply the 4Cs process to Dan's decision. As we do, you will be able to translate it to moral choices you make every day. And you will be able to identify ways you can pass it on to the next generation.

Consider the Choice

What Dan was doing in that chemistry final was evaluating the rightness or wrongness of his action based on the immediate benefits each action offered. That's only natural, of course.

What are some of the short-term benefits Dan might enjoy as a result of copying Stephanie's answers? List three.

1. _____

2. _____

3. _____

What are some short-term consequences Dan might face if he hadn't copied Stephanie's answers? List three.

1. _____

2. _____

3. _____

Do the short-term benefits make Dan's decision right?

❏ Yes, because _____

_____

❏ No, because _____

_____

You see, the number one enemy to the next generation believing in absolutes is selfish justification. That's why Dan made the fundamental mistake of letting his situation cloud his judgment of right and wrong. He tried to judge right and wrong (which is objective) by his experience (which was subjective).

Turn back to the list of things going through Dan's head. Place a check in the box by each one that reveals a reliance on an objective, universal, and constant standard of truth.

The first step in making right choices—consider the choice—can immediately clear a mind clouded by a confusing and unpleasant situation. It exposes the rationalizations and justifications that lead to wrong choices. It can remind you that your choice is not between what you think is right and what you think is wrong; it's between what is objectively right and what is objectively wrong, regardless of what you think.

Keeping that in mind, how would this first step in the 4Cs clarify Dan's many considerations and justifications? If Dan were to consider the choice, how would that affect his decision-making process?

Dan says ...	If Dan considers the choice, he might conclude...
My mom is sick. She couldn't stand it if I fail.	*I am basing this on self-pity, not that it is wrong to cheat.*
I know the answers but my stress and fatigue are keeping me from remembering just now.	_____ _____ _____
Stephanie believes it's OK for me to cheat. She understands my situation.	_____ _____ _____
My teacher isn't looking. I won't get caught, so no one will know or get hurt.	_____ _____ _____
I've gotten good grades and not cheated up to now. Besides, I deserve a good grade.	_____ _____ _____

Another Dan

The Bible contains the story of another Dan who faced a difficult decision in an awkward situation. He and his Jewish friends were expected to eat what everyone else in the Babylonian palace ate ... but the palace served food that God had forbidden.

Read Daniel 1:1-20 below and on the following page.

¹In the third year of the reign of Jehoiakim king of Judah, Nebuchadnezzar king of Babylon came to Jerusalem and besieged it. ²And the Lord delivered Jehoiakim king of Judah into his hand, along with some of the articles from the temple of God. These he carried off to the temple of his god in Babylonia and put in the treasure house of his god.

³Then the king ordered Ashpenaz, chief of his court officials, to bring in some of the Israelites from the royal family and the nobility—⁴young men without any physical defect, handsome, showing aptitude for every kind of learning, well informed, quick to understand, and qualified to serve in the king's palace. He was to teach them the language and literature of the Babylonians. ⁵The king assigned them a daily amount of food and wine from the king's table. They were to be trained for three years, and after that they were to enter the king's service.

⁶Among these were some from Judah: Daniel, Hananiah, Mishael and Azariah. ⁷The chief official gave them new

names: to Daniel, the name Belteshazzar; to Hananiah, Shadrach; to Mishael, Meshach; and to Azariah, Abednego.

⁸But Daniel resolved not to defile himself with the royal food and wine, and he asked the chief official for permission not to defile himself this way. ⁹Now God had caused the official to show favor and sympathy to Daniel, ¹⁰but the official told Daniel, "I am afraid of my lord the king, who has assigned your food and drink. Why should he see you looking worse than the other young men your age? The king would then have my head because of you."

¹¹Daniel then said to the guard whom the chief official had appointed over Daniel, Hananiah, Mishael and Azariah, ¹²"Please test your servants for ten days: Give us nothing but vegetables to eat and water to drink. ¹³Then compare our appearance with that of the young men who eat the royal food, and treat your servants in accordance with what you see." ¹⁴So he agreed to this and tested them for ten days.

¹⁵At the end of the ten days they looked healthier and better nourished than any of the young men who ate the royal food. ¹⁶So the guard took away their choice food and the wine they were to drink and gave them vegetables instead.

¹⁷To these four young men God gave knowledge and understanding of all kinds of literature and learning. And Daniel could understand visions and dreams of all kinds.

¹⁸At the end of the time set by the king to bring them in, the chief official presented them to Nebuchadnezzar. ¹⁹The king talked with them, and he found none equal to Daniel, Hananiah, Mishael and Azariah; so they entered the king's service. ²⁰In every matter of wisdom and understanding about which the king questioned them, he found them ten times better than all the magicians and enchanters in his whole kingdom.

What thoughts might have dominated Daniel's head as he decided what he and his friends should do?

_____

_____

_____

Do you think Daniel tried to judge right and wrong by his experience? ❑ Yes ❑ No

Do you think he considered the choice as being between what was objectively right and what was objectively wrong, regardless of what he thought or felt? ❑ Yes ❑ No

Consider Yourself and the Next Generation

If you could buy a special pair of glasses that allowed you to look into the heads of the children or youth in your life, what would it reveal? Would it show that they: (check any that apply)
- ❏ make decisions based on the immediate benefits?
- ❏ act according to what's in it for them?
- ❏ try to judge right and wrong by their experience, according to each situation?
- ❏ make choices based on an objective, universal, constant standard of right and wrong?

What about you? Review the list above and circle any statements that express the way you make choices.

If you sincerely want to make a difference in the lives of youth, you must not only tell youth how to make right choices, choices that will please God and truly benefit them, you must also be sure your decision-making models the truth. How do you do that? You: C _____ the C _____. Stop and ask yourself, "Who determines what is right or wrong in this situation?" Considering the choice means dismissing your own rationalizations and justifications, and reminding yourself that an absolute standard of truth exists, regardless of your own opinions, feelings, and attitudes.

If you are willing to continue in the process of submitting to God, who alone decides right and wrong, conclude today's study with the following prayer.

> *Father God, I admit that I have been relying on myself to judge right and wrong. I have been making choices based only on what immediately benefits my selfish interests. I have been allowing my situation to guide my decisions, and then trying to call my choice "right." Help me to begin today to consider the choice, to view each moment of decision as a choice between what is right and what is wrong, independently of what I think or feel. I know I'll need your Holy Spirit's guiding presence to do that, so I again affirm my trust in You. In Jesus' name, amen.*

Compare It to God

Have you ever watched a home movie or video in reverse? It can be hilarious to watch people walking backwards, divers jumping magically out of a swimming pool and onto the diving board, and kids lighting the candles on a birthday cake by inhaling!

Wouldn't it be nice to do the same thing in real life? You could rewind the film of your life and take back that awful thing you said to your co-worker. You could reverse your decision to chaperone the youth group campout. You could save yourself the embarrassment of that pathetic perm you got at Dion's House of Hair.

Of course, real life doesn't have a rewind button. But Dan, the guy who copied Stephanie Andrews' test answer on the chemistry final, isn't real! So we can push rewind for him and examine what might have happened if he had submitted to God, using the 4Cs, instead of trying to make his own decision about right and wrong based solely on his situation.

If Dan had considered the choice, he could have recognized that his choice was not between what he *thought* was right or wrong, but between what *was* right or wrong, independently of his particular situation. He could then have proceeded to the next step in making right choices.

Compare It to God

What would have happened if Dan had compared his choice to the nature and character of God? What could he have learned by tracing his choice through precept and principle to the Person of God?

Precept • Read Leviticus 19:11 below.

   Do not steal. Do not lie. Do not deceive one another.

How do those precepts apply to Dan's situation?

Dan stole from _____ when he

_____.

Dan lied to _____ when he

_____.

Dan deceived _____ when he

_____.

Read Jesus' response to the rich young ruler's question about eternal life in Mark 10:19 and add the phrase that applies to Dan's situation:

> You know the commandments: "Do not murder, do not commit adultery, do not steal, do not give false testimony, do not _____, honor your father and mother."

Read the following verses and circle the two-word phrase that appears in each verse.

> Deacons, likewise, are to be men worthy of respect, sincere, not indulging in much wine, and not pursuing dishonest gain (1 Timothy 3:8).

> Since an overseer is entrusted with God's work, he must be blameless—not overbearing, not quick-tempered, not given to much wine, not violent, not pursuing dishonest gain. They must be silenced, because they are ruining whole households by teaching things they ought not to teach— and that for the sake of dishonest gain (Titus 1:7, 11).

How do those verses apply to Dan's situation? _____

_____

Principle • What positive principle lies behind each of those precepts? In other words, what attribute does God want us to possess that such behavior would contradict? Check the principle in the following list.

- ❏ honesty   ❏ trustworthiness
- ❏ pride   ❏ purity
- ❏ commitment   ❏ loyalty

Proverbs 12:22 refers to this principle. Circle the word that states the principle.

> The Lord detests lying lips, but he delights in men who are truthful.

Person • What is it, then, about God that the precepts and the principle point to? Is there something in God's nature and character that would make Dan's decision to copy Stephanie's answers wrong?

Read the following verses and complete the statement that follows.

> O Sovereign LORD, you are God! Your words are trustworthy, and you have given this good promise to your servant (2 Samuel 7:28).

God is _____.

> The man who has accepted it has certified that God is truthful (John 3:33).

God is _____.

> Into your hands I commit my spirit; redeem me, O LORD, the God of truth (Psalm 31:5).

God is the God of _____.

Our challenge as adults is to live a life that models the 4Cs process so that the next generation will know how to use it also. If Dan's head were filled with the 4Cs instead of the confusing and competing thoughts and feelings prompted by his situation, he would be able to see that to copy Stephanie's answers would be wrong, regardless of how tired he is, how life is treating him, or Stephanie's willingness to help. Dan's action would be wrong because, if you compare it to God, you will discover that:

- God's precepts forbid dishonest gain.
- God's precepts forbid dishonest gain because God values honesty and trustworthiness.
- God values honesty and trustworthiness because God is trustworthy and true.

Because God is true, lying is an offense against His nature. Because God is true, cheating is an affront to Him. Because God is true, stealing is an insult to Him. God is true, and there is nothing false in Him. It is His nature, therefore, that defines honesty as moral, and dishonesty, fraud, and theft as evil.

The Test of Truth grounds the virtue of honesty in the nature and character of God. Honesty is good and right—objectively and absolutely—because God is true. Dishonesty is evil and wrong—objectively and universally—because it is contrary to God's character. That is what makes dishonesty wrong—and honesty right—for all people, for all times, and for all places (*Right From Wrong*, 173-174).

Write in the margin the Scripture memory verse, 1 Chronicles 29:17. Ask God to help you memorize these words and apply them to your life.

The Pause Button

If you could rewind the tape of your life, would you reverse a recent moral decision you've made? ❑ Yes ❑ No

How would you see things differently if you consider the choice in that situation and compare it to God?

_____

_____

_____

Take a few moments to pray, committing that situation to God, asking Him for forgiveness (if necessary), and asking Him to guide you in future decisions.

Commit to God's Way

DAY FOUR

Dan dashed into his chemistry final and slid into his seat just as the tardy bell rang. He breathed a weary sigh.

Suddenly, a spooky feeling rushed over him, an overwhelming sense of *déjà vu*. He felt as if someone had just punched some sort of cosmic rewind button. He felt as if he were reliving today's events.

The eerie feeling continued as Mr. Henderson distributed the four-page chemistry final with directions to keep the test face-down on the desk until he gave the signal to begin.

Dan found it difficult to concentrate on the test. *I know this stuff*, he told himself, but his sense that something weird was happening (along with fatigue from having spent so much time with his sick mother at the hospital) clouded his mind until he was convinced he would fail the exam.

He was beginning page three when Stephanie Andrews dropped a page from her test. It floated into the aisle and landed on the floor beside his chair. Now he *knew* something strange was going on; this had all happened to him before, he was sure of it.

He glanced at Stephanie; she seemed not to notice, but something in the movement of her head suggested that the dropped page had not been an accident. He was convinced that she intended for him to see her answers.

It would be so easy. His eyes settled on Stephanie's neat handwriting. He could read the answers without difficulty. His gaze returned to the blank spaces on his own test paper.

Dan's sense of *déjà vu* evaporated, however, when he closed his eyes to think. He considered what he was tempted to do, reminding himself that whatever he did, there was a right thing to do and a wrong thing to do.

In a moment, he remembered that God had forbidden lying and cheating; he couldn't recall any specific verse of Scripture, but he knew that God valued honesty and integrity—because God Himself was faithful and true.

Dan's mouth closed tightly as he realized—beyond a shadow of a doubt—that copying Stephanie's answers would be the wrong thing to do.

But, he told himself, *if I do the right thing, I could flunk the exam—and the course. And I sure don't want that to happen.*

Unlike the rest of us, Dan has a second chance to make the right choice. But even though we've rewound the tape of his life, and even though he's considered the choice and compared it to God, he's not "home free"; Dan still must commit to God's way.

What might committing to God's way involve for Dan in his situation? Check all that you think apply.

- ❏ a quick prayer to God
- ❏ a long prayer to God
- ❏ return the paper to Stephanie
- ❏ copy Stephanie's answers
- ❏ copy someone else's answers
- ❏ ask Mr. Henderson for hints
- ❏ ask God for hints
- ❏ try his hardest to pass the test on his own merits
- ❏ feign sickness
- ❏ feign death
- ❏ plan to take chemistry in summer school if necessary
- ❏ protest to the school board Mr. Henderson's stupid rule
- ❏ explain his mother's situation to Mr. Henderson and ask for a chance to re-take the exam or complete extra work to improve his grade
- ❏ explain his mother's situation and offer to wash Mr. Henderson's car for the rest of his life
- ❏ resolve to do the right thing if it benefits him
- ❏ resolve to do the right thing regardless of the benefits or consequences

If Dan is to make the right choice, he must ... *admit* that his choice is a choice between right and wrong, ... *submit* to God as the authority who determines what is right or wrong, and ... *commit* to God's way by conforming to what God says is right, regardless of the benefits or consequences.

Write in the margin the Scripture memory verse, 1 Chronicles 29:17. Say it aloud five times.

Do you accept this verse? ❏ Yes ❏ No ❏ Undecided

Ask God not only to help you memorize this verse but also to apply it.

Another Daniel, Another Test

Reread Daniel 1:1-20 on pages 102-103. Do you see any similarities between Daniel's situation (in the Bible) and Dan's temptation (in this book)? List the parallels below and on the next page.

Dan   Daniel

_____   _____

_____   _____

_____   _____

_____   _____

_____   _____

How would Dan's situation have ended if he had committed to God's way, like Daniel did? Write a new ending to Dan's story below.

_____

_____

_____

_____

_____

_____

_____

What situation in your life would have ended differently if you had committed to God's way? Briefly describe it below.

_____

_____

_____

Have you already committed to submitting to God, either in the group session or during your daily sessions with this workbook? ❑ Yes ❑ No

If you have already made such a commitment, renew it now, perhaps repeating the "manifesto" you composed on page 84 as a prayer to God.

If you have not made such a commitment, do so now. Admit God's sovereignty, and submit your will to Him, using David's classic prayer from Psalm 51:1-6, 10-12 below. Pray this prayer for yourself putting your name in each blank.

> Have mercy on _____, O God, according to your unfailing love; according to your great compassion blot out _____ transgressions. Wash away _____ iniquity and cleanse _____ from my sin. For I know _____ transgressions, and _____ sin is always before _____. Against you, you only, have _____ sinned

and done what is evil in your sight, so that you are proved right when you speak and justified when you judge. Surely _____ was sinful at birth, sinful from the time my mother conceived _____. Surely you desire truth in the inner parts; you teach _____ wisdom in the inmost place.

Create in _____ a pure heart, O God, and renew a steadfast spirit within _____. Do not cast _____ from your presence or take your Holy Spirit from _____. Restore to _____ the joy of your salvation and grant _____ a willing spirit, to sustain _____. Amen.

Teach this prayer to your children and youth. Memorize it together and invite them to pray it when confessing attitudes and behaviors that are wrong in God's sight.

How would you present a challenge to submit to God to a young person in your life? Script below your challenge to make a commitment to submit to God.

_____

_____

_____

_____

Present this challenge to one young person this week. Pray for wisdom and timing, and that God will be honored in the commitment.

Count on God's Protection and Provision

DAY FIVE

Dan sighed and leaned forward to pick Stephanie's test paper off the floor. He extended it toward her without looking at it.

Stephanie turned and met his gaze. She accepted the page without speaking.

Dan struggled through the exam, working hard to concentrate, skipping portions of the test that mystified him and concentrating his energies on areas in which he felt the most confident. He remained at his desk after most students—including Stephanie— had turned in their tests. He checked his work and attempted to complete the portions he'd skipped earlier.

Dan found out two days later that he had flunked the exam. He went to Mr. Henderson and begged him to waive his rule, or let him re-take the exam; the teacher refused both requests.

Dan sat beside his mother's hospital bed, wondering if he should have just copied Stephanie's answers and saved himself all this trouble. He knew now that he would have passed the test with that little bit of help.

Dan looked at his mother sleeping, and shook his head. He had flunked one test, he realized, but he had passed another.

Counting On God's Protection and Provision

What were the immediate results of Dan's right choice? List them below.

_____

_____

_____

Are the results immediately ❑ positive or ❑ negative? Check one.

The last of the 4Cs, you'll remember, is to Count on God's Protection and Provision. What kinds of protection and provision could possibly result from Dan's choice above?

_____

_____

Dan may not instantly realize many of the benefits of making the right choice, but if he commits to God's way and then counts on His loving protection and provision—even thanking God in faith before he sees any fruits of his obedience—Dan will experience a much happier and healthier future. Why?

• *God's standard of honesty provides a clear conscience, and an unbroken fellowship with God.* If Dan had cheated on his chemistry final, he would have damaged his walk with God. With every right choice, Dan enriches his relationship with God.

• *God's standard of honesty protects from guilt.* Guilt is among the most powerful of emotions, and it will cling to the dishonest heart like a python, choking the life out of its victim. The psalmist David realized that, and expressed it in Psalm 38:4.

My guilt has overwhelmed me like a burden too heavy to bear.

Because Dan committed to God's way, he is protected from the burden of guilt.

• *God's standard of honesty provides a sense of accomplishment that the dishonest heart will never enjoy.* It may take longer and involve sacrifice, but when Dan finally passes chemistry, it will be an accomplishment of which he can be proud because it will belong only to him.

• *God's standard of honesty protects from shame.* What would have happened if Dan had tried to copy Stephanie's answers and been caught? Even if he hadn't been caught, would Stephanie have respected him more or less for what he did? Dan will never have to find out, because his choice protects him from shame.

• *God's standard of honesty provides a reputation for integrity.* Dan may not realize it, but every time he makes a moral choice, he is building a reputation (either a good one or a bad one). Choosing God's way builds a reputation for integrity. Proverbs 22:1 tells us about the value of having a good reputation.

A good name is more desirable than great riches; to be esteemed is better than silver or gold.

When we consider the choice, compare it to God, and commit to God's way, we can count on all the benefits of God's protection and provision.

Daniel's Band of Friends

Reread Daniel 1:1-13 on pages 102-103. Was Daniel counting on God's provision and protection? ❑ Yes ❑ No If so, why?

_____

_____

Reread Daniel 1:14-16 on page 103. Did God's provision fulfill Daniel's expectations? ❑ Yes ❑ No If so, how?

_____

_____

_____

Reread Daniel 1:17-20 on page 103. What long-term benefits did Daniel and his friends enjoy, in addition to passing their ten-day test?

_____

_____

_____

_____

Beginning Now

Write from memory the four steps for making right choices below.

C _____

C _____

C _____

C_____

What would happen if you (and, of course, the children and youth you wish to influence) began _now_ to choose God's way and count on His protection and provision? Check all that apply (continued on the next page).
   ❑ God would disappoint me.
   ❑ God would make me miserable.
   ❑ God would protect me.

❏ God would embarrass me.
❏ God would provide for me.
❏ God would make me sorry I trusted Him.

Which of the above do you think the young people in your life would check if they were to be totally honest? How can you more effectively communicate God's loving motivation (to protect and provide) to them? Be specific and list three actions you will take in the coming days.

1. _____

2. _____

3. _____

Use the following words (based on Psalm 26:2-3) as a model to guide you in prayer to God. Change it to express your own thoughts and feelings.

> *Test me, O Lord, and try me today. Examine my heart and mind, and help me to be honest with You and with myself today. Your love is ever before me, and I thank You because Your motivation is always to protect me and provide for me. I want to walk continually in Your truth. Overcome all the obstacles in my heart and mind, and let me submit to You completely and commit to Your way, not my own. In Jesus' name, amen.*

WEEKLY JOURNAL

I learned that _____

_____

_____

One attitude I had which changed was _____

_____

_____

God spoke to me by _____

_____

_____

One behavior that I will examine is _____

_____

_____

When I shared with the child or youth in my life, _____

_____

_____

The most difficult thing was _____

_____

_____

It was a joy to _____

_____

_____

Tomorrow I will _____

_____

_____

My Scripture memory verse is _____

_____

The Love Connection

In the '50s, the shocking moves and music of a singer named Elvis Presley became a hot topic among preachers.

In the '60s, preachers were often asked what they thought about the "Jesus movement," in which large numbers of "hippies" and (believe it or not) "yippies" began professing faith in Christ.

In the '70s and '80s, many preachers were asked for their reactions to the fortunes and failures of television evangelists.

In Jesus' day, the hot topic of the day was none of the above. They didn't know who Elvis Presley was. They'd never heard of hippies, and there were no televangelists. The question that made the rounds of teachers and preachers of Jesus' time was: "Which is the greatest commandment?"

An expert in the Law once came to Jesus with that question. He was a Pharisee. Pharisees were a religious group of people who knew the commandments inside and out; they believed that there was a commandment to cover every detail of life.

> "Teacher," the man said, "which is the greatest commandment in the Law?"
> Jesus replied, " 'Love the Lord your God with all your heart and with all your soul and with all your mind.' This is the first and greatest commandment. And the second is like it: 'Love your neighbor as yourself.' All the Law and the Prophets hang on these two commandments" (Matthew 22:36-40).

In other words, Jesus was saying that everything God has revealed to us about right and wrong—all the dos and don'ts of His commandments, all the shalts and shalt-nots—are simply explanation and amplification of His command to love.

That question—"Which is the greatest commandment?"—and Jesus' answer will be crucial to your discoveries and decisions this week as you continue to apply the 4Cs process to the choices and challenges you and the children and youth you influence must face every day.

This week you will—
- learn how to apply the 4Cs to choices involving interpersonal conflicts and relationships;
- discover how to apply the precepts and principles of God's Word to those areas;
- uncover the loving nature of God; and
- explore how to model and teach God's love to children and youth.

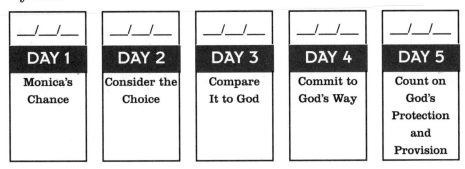

(Add the day/month/year to indicate when you complete your study.)

A key verse to memorize

God is love. Whoever lives in love lives in God, and God in him (1 John 4:16).

Concepts you will come to understand
- Right conduct in interpersonal relationships is rooted in the nature of the God of love.
- The long-term benefits of God's protection and provision outweigh the short-term appeal of unloving actions and attitudes.
- We must admit our unloving attitudes and behaviors and submit to God's way of relating to others.

This Week's Assignments
- Memorize 1 John 4:16.
- Complete daily exercises.
- Use every opportunity you can this week to evaluate prime-time television depictions of "love" with your children or teenagers. During commercials, turn the sound off and "walk through" the 4Cs, relating them to situations depicting love or the lack of biblical love.
- Especially with younger children, recognize and reinforce loving habits this week. Recognize such actions as reflections of God's nature. You might say, "You remind me of God when you show love to your brother," or "I saw how you treated Mrs. Sparks today. You did the right thing, because you acted just like the God of love would want you to act."
- Complete your Weekly Journal.

DAY ONE

Monica's Chance

Monica turned to her mother and screamed, "Stop the car!" Mrs. Jackson slammed her foot on the brakes, watching in the rear-view mirror as a rusty brown pickup truck stopped just in time to avoid a collision. She turned to her daughter, who sat beside her in the front seat.

"What's wrong?" Mrs. Jackson expected Monica to say they had almost run over an animal, but Monica pressed her face against the window and pointed at the line outside the movie theater.

"That's Jimmy," she whispered, "in line with Susan Brock."

Mrs. Jackson's eyes widened. "You mean I almost had an accident because you saw some old boyfriend going to the movies with someone else?" Monica's mother was instantly annoyed with her daughter. This teenage obsession with Jimmy had gone too far; it had been months since Monica claimed that her friend, Gina Price, had stolen Jimmy away from Monica. Jimmy and Gina had been going together ever since. "Monica Jackson!" she huffed at her daughter. "Don't ever do that to me again. Do you hear me?"

"Yeah, Mom," Monica muttered, still watching Jimmy and Susan. "I'm sorry."

Mrs. Jackson peered beyond Monica at the line outside the movie theater; Jimmy did appear to be in line at the movies with pretty Susan Brock. She began to pull the car back into traffic and did not notice—though Monica did—that Jimmy, who was ahead of Susan in line, had turned away from her and was now talking with Nate and Alex, two of his closest buddies. Monica saw that Jimmy was there with his friends, and Susan was accompanied by her parents. They weren't there together at all.

Too bad, she thought as she turned around and settled back into the seat. *Then Gina would know how it feels to have someone steal your boyfriend.*

An idea began to form in Monica's head. After all, she *did* see Jimmy at the movies with Susan. It wouldn't be lying to tell her former friend what she saw. And if she assumed that Jimmy was going out on her…. She smiled. It was a golden opportunity. Besides, she needs to know how bad she hurt me. Then maybe she'd think twice before doing it again.

Monica's Choice

Monica is not planning to lie to her former friend. She's simply planning to tell Gina that she saw Jimmy and Susan standing in line together at the movies.

Perhaps you have been in a situation like Monica's in which a family member or friend did something unkind to you. Briefly describe your experience.

_____

_____

Based on your experience, is Monica's reaction typical?
❏ Yes ❏ No

Do you think children's and teenagers' interpersonal conflicts would be more severe, less severe, or about the same as your struggles as an adult? ❏ More ❏ Less ❏ About the same
Why?

_____

_____

Are any of the young people in your life struggling to discern right from wrong in their interpersonal relationships?
❏ Yes ❏ No

If so, list below the things you think they're struggling with.

_____

_____

Word to the Wise

Of course there's no Bible verse that says, "Thou shalt not tell thy friend that thou sawest the boyfriend thy friend stole from thee standing in line at the movie theater with another girl."

How do you decide, then, the right choice in a situation like Monica's? After all, it can't be wrong to tell a former friend the plain truth, can it? Besides, Monica's plan could teach Gina a valuable lesson.

If you have a study Bible or one with a concordance, use the concordance or topical index to help you answer the following questions.

What are some Bible verses that might apply to Monica's situation? Look up words like *lie, deceit,* and *falsehood.*

_____

_____

What are some biblical concepts or principles that might apply?

_____

_____

As you prepare for this week's study, it is crucial that you be honest and realistic about what choices you would make (or have made)—and why. Remember, you can't effectively communicate accurate standards of right and wrong if you don't model them. Check any statements below that are true of you.

❑ I have done something similar, such as when I _____
_____
❑ I would never do something like what Monica is planning.
❑ I would probably feel like doing it, but I wouldn't go ahead with it.
❑ I would do whatever was easiest.
❑ I would do it, but I would feel badly about it.
❑ I would do it, and I probably wouldn't feel badly about it at all.
❑ I would do it and be proud of it.
❑ I would ask God to forgive me if I were doing wrong.
❑ I would ask God to help keep me from doing wrong.

What does God think about your answers? Is He pleased with all your interpersonal relationships? Do you think He wishes any of your answers were different? Is His Holy Spirit prodding your heart and your conscience about any of your answers? Write your thoughts below.

_____

_____

_____

Pray the words of Psalm 139:23-24 as you prepare your heart and mind for the coming week's studies and discoveries.

Search me, O God, and know my heart; test me and know my anxious thoughts. See if there is any offensive way in me, and lead me in the way everlasting.

Consider the Choice

Mrs. Jackson doesn't yet know what Monica is planning, of course. But even if she did, how could she blame Monica? After all, she knows how Gina hurt her daughter. It would be different, of course, if Gina had never done anything to her, right? It's like a game of chess, and Monica figures it's just her turn.

Put yourself in Monica's shoes. Would it be very difficult to say that giving Gina a taste of her own medicine was wrong?

After all, Monica has some justification for her plan. List the things below that (perhaps more so to a young mind) would make Monica's plan seem right.

_____

_____

_____

Perhaps Monica will enjoy some immediate benefits as a result of her plan. What would such benefits be?

_____

_____

Do those benefits make Monica's plan right?

❑ Yes, because _____

_____

❑ No, because _____

_____

Monica is trying to judge right and wrong (which is objective) by her *emotions* (which are subjective). She is letting her feelings cloud her judgment of right and wrong.

Rather than justifying her actions and proclaiming them "right" because of what Gina has done to her, Monica would be much better off to consider the choice, remembering that her choice is not between what she thinks is right or what she thinks is wrong, but between what *is* right or wrong, regardless of what she thinks.

Write in the margin 1 John 4:16. Say it aloud three times. Ask God to fill you with His love.

David's Move

Monica is not the first to face such a tempting opportunity. The Bible tells the story of David, who had been wronged by a former friend named Saul. In fact, Saul had actually tried to kill David (1 Samuel 18:10-11; 19:1).

Read 1 Samuel 26:1-25 below and answer the questions that follow.

¹The Ziphites went to Saul at Gibeah and said, "Is not David hiding on the hill of Hakilah, which faces Jeshimon?"

²So Saul went down to the Desert of Ziph, with his three thousand chosen men of Israel, to search there for David. ³Saul made his camp beside the road on the hill of Hakilah facing Jeshimon, but David stayed in the desert. When he saw that Saul had followed him there, ⁴he sent out scouts and learned that Saul had definitely arrived.

⁵Then David set out and went to the place where Saul had camped. He saw where Saul and Abner son of Ner, the commander of the army, had lain down. Saul was lying inside the camp, with the army encamped around him.

⁶David then asked Ahimelech the Hittite and Abishai son of Zeruiah, Joab's brother, "Who will go down into the camp with me to Saul?"

"I'll go with you," said Abishai.

⁷So David and Abishai went to the army by night, and there was Saul, lying asleep inside the camp with his spear stuck in the ground near his head. Abner and the soldiers were lying around him.

⁸Abishai said to David, "Today God has delivered your enemy into your hands. Now let me pin him to the ground with one thrust of my spear; I won't strike him twice."

⁹But David said to Abishai, "Don't destroy him! Who can lay a hand on the LORD's anointed and be guiltless? ¹⁰As surely as the LORD lives," he said, "the LORD himself will strike him; either his time will come and he will die, or he will go into battle and perish. ¹¹But the LORD forbid that I should lay a hand on the LORD's anointed. Now get the spear and water jug that are near his head, and let's go."

¹²So David took the spear and water jug near Saul's head, and they left. No one saw or knew about it, nor did anyone wake up. They were all sleeping, because the LORD had put them into a deep sleep.

¹³Then David crossed over to the other side and stood on top of the hill some distance away; there was a wide space between them. ¹⁴He called out to the army and to Abner son of Ner, "Aren't you going to answer me, Abner?"

Abner replied, "Who are you who calls to the king?"

¹⁵David said, "You're a man, aren't you? And who is like you in Israel? Why didn't you guard your lord the king? Someone came to destroy your lord the king. ¹⁶What you have done is not good. As surely as the LORD lives, you and your men deserve to die, because you did not guard your master, the LORD's anointed. Look around you. Where are the king's spear and water jug that were near his head?"

¹⁷Saul recognized David's voice and said, "Is that your voice, David my son?"

David replied, "Yes it is, my lord the king." ¹⁸And he added, "Why is my lord pursuing his servant? What have I done, and what wrong am I guilty of? ¹⁹Now let my lord the king listen to his servant's words. If the Lord has incited you against me, then may he accept an offering. If, however, men have done it, may they be cursed before the LORD! They have now driven me from my share in the LORD's inheritance and have said, 'Go, serve other gods.' ²⁰Now do not let my blood fall to the ground far from the presence of the LORD. The king of Israel has come out to look for a flea—as one hunts a partridge in the mountains."

²¹Then Saul said, "I have sinned. Come back, David my son. Because you considered my life precious today, I will not try to harm you again. Surely I have acted like a fool and have erred greatly."

²²"Here is the king's spear," David answered. "Let one of your young men come over and get it. ²³The LORD rewards every man for his righteousness and faithfulness. The LORD delivered you into my hands today, but I would not lay a hand on the LORD's anointed. ²⁴As surely as I valued your life today, so may the LORD value my life and deliver me from all trouble."

²⁵Then Saul said to David, "May you be blessed, my son David; you will do great things and surely triumph."

So David went on his way, and Saul returned home.

In what ways was David's experience similar to Monica's?
- ❏ each one had been wronged by a close friend
- ❏ each one had an opportunity to gain revenge for a previous misdeed
- ❏ each one shared the attitude that the Lord would take care of the situation
- ❏ each one was more concerned about immediate benefits than long-term consequences

Did David try to judge right and wrong by his *emotions*?
❏ Yes ❏ No

Go back and circle specific portions of the scriptural account to support your conclusion.

Consider Yourself

What about the children and youth in your life? Are they:
- making choices based on immediate benefits?
- justifying decisions about what's right or wrong according to what's in it for them?
- trying to judge right and wrong by their emotions?
- making choices based on a belief in an objective, universal, constant standard of right and wrong?

Review the above questions, asking them of *yourself*.

Anyone who sincerely wants to make right choices, choices that will please God and bring the greatest lasting benefits must begin with the first step of the 4Cs, which is:

C _____ the C _____

As you continue submitting to God through the conscious, consistent practice of the 4Cs, you will be better equipped to guide children and teenagers in a similar process. If that is your desire, conclude today's study in prayer, using the following as a guide.

Father God, I praise You because _____

_____

I want to _____

_____

I ask You to _____

_____

Help me to _____

_____

In Jesus' name, amen.

Compare It to God

Monica said goodnight to her mother and closed her bedroom door. She reached into the drawer of her nightstand, pulled out her diary, and began to write.

> Saw Jimmy in line at the movies today. He was talking to Susan Brock. He was with friends and she was with her parents.
>
> I can't wait to see Gina tomorrow. I'll smile like we're still friends and tell her that I saw the two of them in line together at the movies. I'll tell her how pretty Susan looked and how close they were standing. That ought to give Gina something to think about. With any luck, she'll throw one of her temper tantrums around Jimmy. He'll finally see what she's *really* like. Maybe they'll even get mad and break up.
>
> The best part of it is, I'll only be telling the truth. I won't be doing anything wrong. Just teaching my former best friend a lesson.

Monica is still trying to judge the rightness or wrongness of her actions. Asking herself the question, *Who decides what's right or wrong in this situation?* would better equip Monica to recognize that her choice is between objective standards of right and wrong, regardless of her situation or justification. She could then proceed to the next step in making right choices, which is to:

C _____ it to G _____.

The Second C

What would happen if Monica compared her action to the nature and character of God? What would she learn by tracing her choice through precept and principle to the Person of God Himself?

Precept • Read Jesus' words in Matthew 22:36-40.

> ³⁶"Teacher, which is the greatest commandment in the Law?"
> ³⁷Jesus replied: " 'Love the Lord your God with all your heart and with all your soul and with all your mind.' ³⁸This is the first and greatest commandment. ³⁹And the second is like it: 'Love your neighbor as yourself.' ⁴⁰All the Law and the Prophets hang on these two commandments."

How do Jesus' words apply to Monica's situation? _____

Read Matthew 5:43-46 below.

[43]"You have heard that it was said, 'Love your neighbor and hate your enemy.' [44]But I tell you: Love your enemies and pray for those who persecute you, [45]that you may be sons of your Father in heaven. He causes his sun to rise on the evil and the good, and sends rain on the righteous and the unrighteous."[46]If you love those who love you, what reward will you get? Are not even the tax collectors doing that?"

What precept did Jesus quote? Check one.
❑ Do unto others as they do unto you.
❑ Love your enemies and pray for those who persecute you.
❑ Eye for an eye, and tooth for tooth.

How does that precept apply to Monica's situation?_____

_____

God's precepts command us to love and to act in love.

Principle • What positive principle lies behind those precepts?

_____

_____

God's commands us to love because God values love.

Person • What is it, then, about God that the precepts and the principle point to? Is there something in God's nature and character that would make Monica's action toward Gina wrong?

Read the following verses and complete the statement that follows.

Whoever does not love does not know God, because God is love (1 John 4:8).

God is _____

And so we know and rely on the love God has for us. God is love. Whoever lives in love lives in God, and God in him (1 John 4:16).

God is _____

Finally, brothers, good-by. Aim for perfection, listen to my appeal, be of one mind, live in peace. And the God of love and peace will be with you (2 Corinthians 13:11).

God is "the God of _____"

Because God is love, His nature dictates His action. Read the following Scriptures that describe the love of God. After each passage, write a phrase or thought that summarizes how God's loving nature is manifested in action.

The Lord did not set his affection on you and choose you because you were more numerous than other peoples, for you were the fewest of all peoples. But it was because the Lord loved you and kept the oath he swore to your forefathers that he brought you out with a mighty hand and redeemed you from the land of slavery, from the power of Pharaoh king of Egypt (Deuteronomy 7:7-8).

Summary: _____

As a father has compassion on his children, so the Lord has compassion on those who fear him (Psalm 103:13).

Summary: _____

"Surely it was for my benefit
    that I suffered such anguish.
In your love you kept me
    from the pit of destruction;
you have put all my sins
    behind your back" (Isaiah 38:17).

Summary: _____

But because of his great love for us, God, who is rich in mercy, made us alive with Christ even when we were dead in transgressions—it is by grace you have been saved (Ephesians 2:4).

Summary: _____

But when the kindness and love of God our Savior appeared, he saved us, not because of righteous things we had done, but because of his mercy. He saved us through the washing of rebirth and renewal by the Holy Spirit (Titus 3:4).

Summary: _____

If anyone has material possessions and sees his brother in need but has no pity on him, how can the love of God be in him? (1 John 3:17).

Summary: _____

God values love because God is love. Write your Scripture memory verse for this week, 1 John 4:16, in the margin.

If Monica were trying to judge right and wrong according to the 4Cs, she would be able to see that her action would be wrong, regardless of how Gina treated her, how much she misses Jimmy, or whether she could accomplish it without lying. Her action would be wrong because, if you compare it to God, you will discover that:
  • God's precepts command us to love and to act in love.
  • God's precepts command us to love because God values love.
  • God values love because God is love.

Monica's attitude and action toward Gina is wrong because it is not loving. It contradicts the nature of God, who is love.

Monica and You

Are there any unloving attitudes in your heart and mind? Are you contemplating or pursuing any actions that are contradictory to God's nature and character? ❑ Yes ❑ No

List below any attitudes that you need to submit to God's standard of love.

My attitude toward _____

My attitude about _____

List below any actions that you need to change, based on God's standard of love.

The way I act toward _____

The way I act when _____

Close today's study with a prayer asking God to reveal to you any actions or attitudes you need to compare to Him.

Commit to God's Way

Monica sat up on the edge of her bed. She cast a glance at the red numbers of her lighted clock. It was 12:10 a.m.

She had been tossing and turning in bed since 10:00. Monica had been thinking about tomorrow, about her plans for Gina, and about Jimmy.

Something was bothering Monica about all this. She turned on the light beside her bed and stared at the poster-covered walls for a few moments. Then she turned her gaze to her desk where her schoolbooks were stacked next to her Bible and her copy of *Setting You Free to Make Right Choices* workbook.

"This is too weird," she thought. "I feel like I'm one of those kids in that workbook." She and her church youth group had been working through the Right From Wrong workbook, learning how to make right choices.

"This is different, though," Monica said, feeling as if she were talking not only to herself, but to Someone else as well. "I mean, I know God said we should love each other, and that love is a big thing to Him because He is love, but this is different."

Monica frowned. "I mean, Jimmy was my boyfriend first. Gina had no right to do what she did." She stood for a moment, then plopped back down on the edge of her bed. "It was wrong for her to do what she did, not for me to do what I'm going to do."

She turned out the light and laid back down on her bed. She closed her eyes, and waited for sleep to come.

Wait a minute! What's happening? It seems like Monica has considered the choice and even compared it to God, yet she's still determined to carry out her plan.

That's because the first two steps toward making right choices require an admission of God's sovereignty; the third step demands submission. And that's where Monica's having trouble. Remember, the number one enemy to young people believing in absolutes is selfish justification. Monica doesn't want to turn from her own selfish ways, so she is finding ways to justify her actions according to her individual situation instead of submitting and committing to God's ways.

Ancient People, Modern Problem

First Samuel 26 contains the story of Saul and David in the Desert of Ziph. Read verses 1-8 below.

¹The Ziphites went to Saul at Gibeah and said, "Is not David hiding on the hill of Hakilah, which faces Jeshimon?" ²So Saul went down to the Desert of Ziph, with his three thousand chosen men of Israel, to search there for David. ³Saul made his camp beside the road on the hill of Hakilah facing Jeshimon, but David stayed in the desert. When he saw that Saul had followed him there, ⁴he sent out scouts and learned that Saul had definitely arrived.

⁵Then David set out and went to the place where Saul had camped. He saw where Saul and Abner son of Ner, the commander of the army, had lain down. Saul was lying inside the camp, with the army encamped around him.

⁶David then asked Ahimelech the Hittite and Abishai son of Zeruiah, Joab's brother, "Who will go down into the camp with me to Saul?"

"I'll go with you," said Abishai.

⁷So David and Abishai went to the army by night, and there was Saul, lying asleep inside the camp with his spear stuck in the ground near his head. Abner and the soldiers were lying around him.

⁸Abishai said to David, "Today God has delivered your enemy into your hands. Now let me pin him to the ground with one thrust of my spear; I won't strike him twice."

Had Saul ever mistreated David? ❑ Yes ❑ No If so, how?

Read verses 9-13 below.

⁹But David said to Abishai, "Don't destroy him! Who can lay a hand on the LORD's anointed and be guiltless? ¹⁰As surely as the LORD lives," he said, "the LORD himself will strike him; either his time will come and he will die, or he will go into battle and perish. ¹¹But the LORD forbid that I should lay a hand on the LORD's anointed. Now get the spear and water jug that are near his head, and let's go."

¹²So David took the spear and water jug near Saul's head, and they left. No one saw or knew about it, nor did anyone wake up. They were all sleeping, because the LORD had put them into a deep sleep.

¹³Then David crossed over to the other side and stood on top of the hill some distance away; there was a wide space between them.

How did David respond to Saul's mistreatment?

❑ David left Saul's fate in the hands of the Lord.
❑ David intervened to save Saul's life.
❑ David destroyed Saul.

Read verses 14-25 below.

¹⁴He called out to the army and to Abner son of Ner, "Aren't you going to answer me, Abner?"

Abner replied, "Who are you who calls to the king?"

¹⁵David said, "You're a man, aren't you? And who is like you in Israel? Why didn't you guard your lord the king? Someone came to destroy your lord the king. ¹⁶What you have done is not good. As surely as the LORD lives, you and your men deserve to die, because you did not guard your master, the LORD's anointed. Look around you. Where are the king's spear and water jug that were near his head?"

¹⁷Saul recognized David's voice and said, "Is that your voice, David my son?"

David replied, "Yes it is, my lord the king." ¹⁸And he added, "Why is my lord pursuing his servant? What have I done, and what wrong am I guilty of? ¹⁹Now let my lord the king listen to his servant's words. If the LORD has incited you against me, then may he accept an offering. If, however, men have done it, may they be cursed before the LORD! They have now driven me from my share in the LORD's inheritance and have said, 'Go, serve other gods.' ²⁰Now do not let my blood fall to the ground far from the presence of the LORD. The king of Israel has come out to look for a flea—as one hunts a partridge in the mountains."

²¹Then Saul said, "I have sinned. Come back, David my son. Because you considered my life precious today, I will not try to harm you again. Surely I have acted like a fool and have erred greatly."

²²"Here is the king's spear," David answered. "Let one of your young men come over and get it. ²³The LORD rewards every man for his righteousness and faithfulness. The LORD delivered you into my hands today, but I would not lay a hand on the LORD's anointed. ²⁴As surely as I valued your life today, so may the LORD value my life and deliver me from all trouble."

²⁵Then Saul said to David, "May you be blessed, my son David; you will do great things and surely triumph."

So David went on his way, and Saul returned home.

Why did David respond the way he did? _____

_____

Read 2 Samuel 1:1-4, 11-12, 17-24 on the following page.

[1]After the death of Saul, David returned from defeating the Amalekites and stayed in Ziklag two days. [2]On the third day a man arrived from Saul's camp, with his clothes torn and with dust on his head. When he came to David, he fell to the ground to pay him honor.

[3]"Where have you come from?" David asked him.

He answered, "I have escaped from the Israelite camp."

[4]"What happened?" David asked. "Tell me."

He said, "The men fled from the battle. Many of them fell and died. And Saul and his son Jonathan are dead."

[11]Then David and all the men with him took hold of their clothes and tore them. [12]They mourned and wept and fasted till evening for Saul and his son Jonathan, and for the army of the Lord and the house of Israel, because they had fallen by the sword.

[17]David took up this lament concerning Saul and his son Jonathan. [18]and ordered that the men of Judah be taught this lament of the bow (it is written in the Book of Jashar):

[19]"Your glory, O Israel, lies slain on your heights.

How the mighty have fallen!

[20]"Tell it not in Gath,

proclaim it not in the streets of Ashkelon,

lest the daughters of the Philistines be glad,

lest the daughters of the uncircumcised rejoice.

[21]"O mountains of Gilboa,

may you have neither dew nor rain,

nor fields that yield offerings [of grain].

For there the shield of the mighty was defiled,

the shield of Saul—no longer rubbed with oil.

[22]From the blood of the slain,

from the flesh of the mighty,

the bow of Jonathan did not turn back,

the sword of Saul did not return unsatisfied.

[23]"Saul and Jonathan—

in life they were loved and gracious,

and in death they were not parted.

They were swifter than eagles,

they were stronger than lions.

[24]"O daughters of Israel,

weep for Saul,

who clothed you in scarlet and finery,

who adorned your garments with ornaments of gold.

How did David respond when he heard of Saul's death?

❑ David lamented for Saul.

❑ David celebrated Saul's death.

❑ David mourned, wept, and fasted.

Read 2 Samuel 2:1-7 below.

¹In the course of time, David inquired of the LORD. "Shall I go up to one of the towns of Judah?" he asked.

The LORD said, "Go up."

David asked, "Where shall I go?"

"To Hebron," the LORD answered.

²So David went up there with his two wives, Ahinoam of Jezreel and Abigail, the widow of Nabal of Carmel. ³David also took the men who were with him, each with his family, and they settled in Hebron and its towns. ⁴Then the men of Judah came to Hebron and there they anointed David king over the house of Judah.

When David was told that it was the men of Jabesh Gilead who had buried Saul, ⁵he sent messengers to the men of Jabesh Gilead to say to them, "The LORD bless you for showing this kindness to Saul your master by burying him. ⁶May the LORD now show you kindness and faithfulness, and I too will show you the same favor because you have done this. ⁷Now then, be strong and brave, for Saul your master is dead, and the house of Judah has anointed me king over them."

How does David's action in these passages compare with God?

_____

_____

How does it compare with Monica's action?

_____

_____

Your Mission

Do you think committing to God's way would be easy for Monica? ❑ Yes ❑ No

What would be most difficult for her? _____

_____

_____

What would be most difficult for her mother or another adult who is trying to lead her to commit to God's way?

_____

What is most difficult for you in committing to God's way?

_____

_____

Suppose you overheard Monica's late-night conversation with herself, and figured out what she was contemplating. What would you do? What would you say to her?

_____

_____

_____

What effect would you realistically hope to have on her attitudes and actions?

_____

_____

_____

Remember that once a person commits to God's way, he or she must depend on God to provide the power to walk in His ways. All of us—young person or adult—lack the power to make right choices on our own consistently; we need God's help.

Have you committed to God's ways? Are you depending on His help? On a separate sheet of paper, list the people in your life whom you are currently finding it most difficult to love. Title it, "Committing to God's Ways To-Do List." What would it mean to commit to God's way in your relationships with them? Write down by each name one loving action you can take this week toward that person; keep the list in your pocket or purse as a reminder.

Close today's study with a prayer renewing your commitment and thanking God for giving you the power to walk in His ways.

Count on God's Protection and Provision

Many adults still recall the movie serials that were popular in the second quarter of the twentieth century. The movies featured regular installments of an ongoing adventure starring an adventurous hero, like cowboy Tom Mix or astronaut Flash Gordon. Many young moviegoers of that era would spend hours between episodes reenacting the past Saturday's cliffhanger and imagining an exciting ending to the hero's dilemma.

If Monica's situation were just such a movie, and you could choose your own adventure for her, how would you end it? Put the finishing touches on the script below by filling in the blanks according to what choice you think she would make, and the benefits or consequences that might result.

[Fade in; Monica's bedroom. Monica rolls out of bed and rubs the sleep out of her eyes.]

MONICA: "I've made my decision." [Trying to sound more determined than she feels.] "I'm going to _____."

[Scene change; show Monica rushing through breakfast, and arriving at school in time to see Gina standing at her locker. Monica eyes her former friend carefully, looking up and down the hall for any sign of Jimmy. When she's confident the coast is clear, she approaches Gina.]

MONICA: [sweetly] "Hi, Gina."

[Gina's eyes widen at Monica's greeting, but she says nothing.]

MONICA: "I've got something I need to tell you. _____

_____

What do you think about that?"

[Gina's eyes cloud with tears as if she can't believe what she is hearing.]

MONICA: "I'll see you later, OK?" [Monica smiles, as if inwardly congratulating herself for the effect her words had obviously had on Gina. She turns and walks down the hall, nearly skipping with self-satisfaction.]

NARRATOR'S VOICE-OVER: "Monica thought about what she had done for the rest of the day. It made her feel _____, knowing that she had _____.
Somehow, in her heart, she knew _____
and from now on, _____.

Count on It

The last of the 4Cs, you'll remember, is to count on God's protection and provision. According to your script, will Monica be able to count on God's protection and provision?
  ❏ Yes, I think so. ❏ No, I'm not sure she can.

Monica may not instantly realize many of the benefits of making the right choice. However, if Monica commits to God's way and then begins to thank Him for His loving protection and provision—even if she never sees any benefits—she will pave the way for a much happier and healthier future. Why?[1]

• *God's standards of love protect from strife and provides for peace.* Have you ever seen a willful two-year-old express his anger by biting himself? Such behavior illustrates the fact that hatred and hostility harms us more than the anyone at whom we may aim our hatred. God knows that unloving attitudes and actions poison our lives and fill us with strife. A life of love toward others is a life of peace.

• *God's standards of love protect from self-centeredness and provides for fulfillment.* Perhaps you know someone who evaluates every conversation, every relationship, every event of life in terms of how it affects him or her. Such a person may have friends and acquaintances without really loving any of them. The person who loves God and others expresses interest in the ideas and pursuits of others, often enjoys giving as much as receiving, and finds joy in sharing with others and caring for them. Such a person naturally tends to be more appreciated than the self-centered individual.

• *God's standards of love protect from spiritual barrenness and provides for spiritual blessing.* John the apostle wrote, "Anyone who does not love remains in death. Anyone who hates his brother is a murderer, and you know that no murderer has eternal life in him" (1 John 3:14-15). Such strong language communicates the tragic spiritual consequences God wants to protect us from; that is why He commands us to love. God wants to protect us from the barrenness of an unloving soul and provide the spiritual blessings that spring from "the most excellent way" (1 Corinthians 12:31) of love.

These are not the only ways that obedience to God's command to love Him and others protects us and provides for us. Fill in the blanks below with other ways.

- God's standards of love protect from _____ and provide for _____.

- God's standards of love protect from _____ and provide for _____.

- God's standards of love protect from _____ and provide for _____.

The King and I

Let's learn once more about David's confrontation with Saul, the first king of Israel. Reread 1 Samuel 26:21-25 on page 133. Paraphrase the words of David that reveal that he was counting on God's protection and provision.

_____

_____

According to the biblical record in 1 Samuel 26:1-25, did David (check all that apply):
❏ consider the choice?
❏ compare it to God?
❏ commit to God's way?
❏ count on God's protection and provision?

Which of the 4Cs presents the greatest struggle for the children and youth in your life?

_____

_____

In which of the 4Cs are you having the most success? _____

_____

Conclude today's study by spending time in prayer, thanking God for your success in that area and confiding in Him about your struggles in other areas. Finally, ask God to use you to guide the children and teenagers through the 4Cs and into right choices.

[1]See *Right From Wrong*, pp. 210-212 for more discussion of the benefits (protection and provision) of God's standard of love.

WEEKLY JOURNAL

I learned that _____

_____

_____

One attitude I had which changed was _____

_____

_____

God spoke to me by _____

_____

_____

One behavior that I will examine is _____

_____

_____

When I shared with the child or youth in my life, _____

_____

_____

The most difficult thing was _____

_____

_____

It was a joy to _____

_____

_____

Tomorrow I will _____

_____

_____

My Scripture memory verse is_____

_____

The Urge to Merge

In December 1962, a London engineer stopped his train in the midst of a lingering fog, a fog that was thick even by London standards. Concluding perhaps that the fog was too thick and his vision too impaired to proceed any farther, the experienced train man opened the door and stepped down from his cab into forty feet of water. The fog was so thick, he had no idea that he had stopped the train on a bridge. The engineer was one of more than 100 Londoners who died that week from fog.

That is not the only tragedy caused by fog. Another kind of fog often endangers young people and adults who must decide between right and wrong in matters pertaining to love and sex.

People of all ages in love often seem to be enveloped in a kind of fog that blurs their sight and clouds their perception of right and wrong. If they are not equipped with strong biblical values, even those who have been raised in the church are likely to make disastrous choices in the area of love and sex.

According to the study, your kids are much more likely to accept sexual petting and intercourse before marriage as moral if they lack a strong pro-truth view. Youth who *do not* affirm the existence of absolute truth are twice as likely to classify fondling of breasts (between unmarried persons) as moral. Our kids who are not equipped with a consistent view of truth and morality are three times as likely to regard fondling of genitals (between unmarried persons) as morally acceptable. And kids who do not accept truth as absolute are four times as likely to approve premarital sexual intercourse as a "moral" choice.

Keep in mind that the data indicate that nearly all of the kids who define a behavior as "morally acceptable" have engaged in it. Consequently, it is likely that those kids who define premarital petting or intercourse as "moral" have succumbed (or will soon) to the temptation to engage in that behavior. Therefore, while a strong foundation of biblical views about truth and morality is no guarantee that your kids will not become sexually involved before marriage, the *lack* of a strong foundation may nearly guarantee that they will! (*Right From Wrong*, 57).

You will see as a result of this week's studies that the 4Cs method for making right choices can clear the fog and provide valuable insight into questions about romantic love and sex for children, youth, and adults.

This week you will—

- learn how to apply the 4Cs to choices about sex;
- discover how to apply the precepts and principles of God's Word to choices about sex;
- uncover the roots of sexual purity and pleasure in the very nature of God; and
- explore how to model and teach God's truth about sexual behavior to children and youth.

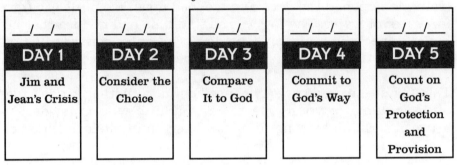

(Add day/month/year to indicate when you complete your study.)

A key verse to memorize

Put to death, therefore, whatever belongs to your earthly nature: sexual immorality [and] impurity ... (Colossians 3:5).

Concepts you will come to understand

- Right sexual behavior (vs. wrong sexual behavior) is defined by the nature of God Himself;
- Only sex that is characterized by love, purity, and faithfulness conforms to God's standard;
- The long-term benefits of God's protection and provision far outweigh the short-term appeal of sexual immorality.

This Week's Assignments

- Memorize Colossians 3:5.
- Complete daily exercises.
- If you're married, use your wedding album as a discussion starter to impress upon your children or teenager(s) why you're married, why your spouse's vows are important to you, and how those vows protect and provide for you.
- Look for opportunities this week to correct the warped portrayal of love and sex in the "entertainment" and print media. Use favorite television shows as springboards for discussion of the 4Cs as they relate to sex. Rent a video (or borrow one from the library) for the express purpose of viewing it with a young person and evaluating the messages about sex that it communicates.
- Complete your Weekly Journal.

DAY ONE

Jim and Jean's Crisis

"I love you," Jim said, his arms entwined around the petite form of his girlfriend, Jean.

"I love you, too," she answered. She leaned backward and soon they were lying together on the couch in Jean's living room.

Jim and Jean had been dating since their sophomore year and had even begun talking about marriage. They were both Christians, but their relationship had lately become more intense than ever, and it seemed nearly impossible now to continue to postpone the inevitable.

"When are your roommates supposed to come home?" Jim asked.

"Late," she answered, understanding the reason for Jim's question. She and Jim loved each other, and she was sure this was the boy she would marry.

Their kisses became more passionate, and they began to do things they had never done before in several years of dating. Neither of them said anything, but both understood they wouldn't "go all the way." They both intended to save that for their wedding night. In fact, that was one of the reasons Jean loved Jim, because he wanted to be a virgin when he got married.

But tonight, each of them reasoned, there was no longer any reason to hold back. What difference could it possibly make? It would be wrong if they didn't love each other, of course. It would be wrong if they weren't serious. It would be wrong to actually have intercourse. But surely, Jim and Jean figured, what they were doing wasn't wrong. Not for them. Not under the circumstances.

"I love you," Jean murmured in Jim's ear.

"I love you, too," he answered.

It Feels So Right

Jim and Jean are in a difficult situation, and their struggle is intensified by emotional and chemical factors. They must contend not only with the intellectual and spiritual issues, but with their passions and their raging hormones.

Those are some of the issues that make choices in the area of love and sex so difficult. Like a thick fog, such powerful emotional and chemical forces can blur your vision and make it even more difficult for guys and girls in love to discern—and choose—right from wrong.

A popular song some years ago contained the line, "It can't be wrong, 'cause it feels so right." That kind of thinking is common among people in love, but it overlooks an important truth: *feelings don't determine what's right or wrong.*

Think back to week one and two. Based on your discoveries in those studies, what determines what's right or wrong?

_____

Look back on Jim and Jean's story on page 144. Circle or highlight words or phrases that refer to their thought processes. Using the graph below, shade each column to reflect how you think each of the four main factors are influencing Jim and Jean's decision. The four columns should add up to 100%.

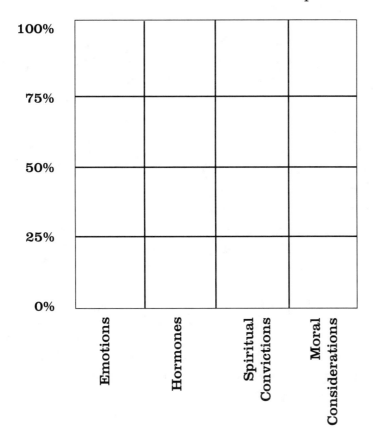

Believe it or not, Jim and Jean are typical. They reflect the beliefs of many adults and young people. And not just young people in general, but churched youth from Christian families.

One in five of our kids (20 percent) said they think sexual intercourse between unmarried persons is morally acceptable; more than twice that number (46 percent) said that they would be more likely to have sex with someone if they "were in love with the person." In other words, nearly half of our kids would tend to agree with [the] attitude that love—not marriage—makes [sex] right.

To many of our kids, that is also true of an intention to marry. Forty-four percent say that they would be more likely to have sex with a person they "really intended to marry." Thus, nearly half of our kids stop short of endorsing the marriage commitment alone as the proper context of sex, but consider the intention to marry (a determination that may pale or disappear tomorrow, or next week, or next month) a suitable incentive for sexual involvement—another indication of our kids' willingness to compromise sexually in advance of marriage.

Similarly, one in four of our kids (26 percent) say that they would be more likely to have sex if they were positive a pregnancy would not result. An identical number responded that they would be more likely to "go all the way" if they could know that their parents would not find out, and one in five (22 percent) said they would be more likely to have sex if they felt that their parents "would not mind." Perhaps the sole encouragement we can glean from the data is that only one in nine (11 percent) said that being "strongly encouraged" by friends to have sex would make them more likely to do so. ...

Such responses reveal that our kids' morals are not based on fundamental, fixed principles, but on fluid concepts of right and wrong. As a result, our children's decisions about the morality and advisability of sexual involvement are subject chiefly to their youthful emotions or intentions. There has not been a significant change in how our youth responded to this set of questions from 1987. ...

These statistics point out the fact that our youth are floundering and flailing; they are being tempted and tossed because they do not have a sound moral and spiritual standard to anchor them when they are faced with difficult choices. As we will see, that single factor—the possession of a strong truth view—will make a world of difference in what they think and do (*Right From Wrong*, 274).

Chapter and Verse

Jim and Jean are Christians, and they usually have no trouble determining right from wrong. They just figure in this case that things are different for them than for most couples.

Are they right? After all, they love each other, don't they? They're serious. They're thinking about marriage. And it's not like they're *planning* to "go all the way."

What are some Bible verses that might apply to their situation? If you have a study Bible or a Bible with a concordance, use the concordance or topical index to help you answer.

_____

_____

What are some biblical concepts or principles that might apply?

_____

_____

Of course, many parents and leaders feel hampered in this area because they themselves did not abstain from premarital sexual involvement. Do you think that disqualifies a person from speaking with authority about love and sex?
  ❏ Yes ❏ No ❏ I don't know Why or why not? _____

_____

_____

Do you apply that reasoning to areas other than sex (in other words, do you shy from teaching right from wrong in areas where you have failed personally, such as love or honesty)?
  ❏ Yes ❏ No ❏ I don't know Explain your answer.

_____

_____

Of course, some adults have difficulty addressing this issue with young people for several reasons. Do any of the following reflect how you feel? Don't miss the options on the next page.
  ❏ I'm embarrassed to talk about sexual things.
  ❏ I'm uncomfortable because of my own premarital sexual activity.
  ❏ I'm not so sure about what's right and what's wrong in this area myself.
  ❏ I'm afraid of the questions kids may ask.
  ❏ It's not my place.
  ❏ I don't think it's as big a deal as everyone says.

❑ I just haven't found the right opportunity.
❑ I don't think my kids are ready to talk about such things.
❑ I'm afraid I might encourage them to become sexually active.
❑ Other _____

You may need to resolve your feelings of inadequacy by getting help through personal study, counseling, or discussions with other adults.

Close today's study with a prayer, using the following pattern:
• Praise God for who He is,
• Thank God for what He does,
• Ask God to lead you to discern and do what is right as you submit yourself to Him and commit yourself to His ways. Ask God to help you guide youth and children to do the same.

Consider the Choice

Jean closed her eyes as she returned Jim's passionate kiss. Her heart felt as though it were beating a thousand times a minute, and she felt suddenly out of breath. She and Jim struggled against the crowded confines of the couch and the constraints of their clothing.

"Ow!" she said, as Jim's elbow pinned her hair to the couch cushion.

"I'm sorry," he cooed. "Are you all right?"

"Yes," she answered. "Just move your elbow."

He shifted his weight and then closed his eyes and leaned in to kiss her again. She did not close her eyes, but cast a wary eye at the clock on the mantel. She didn't want to lose track of time. Her roommates could return home as early as midnight.

Jim and Jean have resisted the temptation to engage in premarital sex or heavy petting for several years now, yet they are giving in to their passions now. Why? List the issues below that you think have prompted their decision to become more physically involved.

_____

_____

Do Jim and Jean expect to enjoy some immediate benefits as a result of their decision? What would such benefits be?

_____

Do those things make their behavior *right*?

❑ Yes, because _____

_____

❑ No, because _____

_____

Jim and Jean are trying to judge right and wrong by their passions. They are letting their raging hormones cloud their judgment of right and wrong.

What *should* they do rather than justifying their actions and proclaiming them "right" because of their plans and passions?

C _____ the C _____

Remember, the number one enemy to believing in absolutes (and making right choices) is selfish justification. That is exactly where Jim and Jean are stumbling; they are *justifying what they want to do*, not *asking what they should do*. If they were to consider the choice, however, they would remember that their choice is not between _____ and _____, but between _____ and _____ regardless of what they think.

Write three times in the margin Colossians 3:5, the Scripture memory verse. Ask God to help you memorize and apply this verse.

A King-Sized Bed

Second Samuel 11 contains the story of David, and a horribly wrong choice he made.

Read 2 Samuel 11:1-17, 26-27 below.

¹In the spring, at the time when kings go off to war, David sent Joab out with the king's men and the whole Israelite army. They destroyed the Ammonites and besieged Rabbah. But David remained in Jerusalem.
²One evening David got up from his bed and walked around on the roof of the palace. From the roof he saw a woman bathing. The woman was very beautiful, ³and David sent someone to find out about her. The man said, "Isn't this Bathsheba, the daughter of Eliam and the wife of Uriah the Hittite?" ⁴Then David sent messengers to get her. She came to him, and he slept with her. (She had purified herself from her uncleanness.) Then she went back home. ⁵The woman conceived and sent word to David, saying, "I am pregnant."
⁶So David sent this word to Joab: "Send me Uriah the Hittite." And Joab sent him to David. ⁷When Uriah came to him, David asked him how Joab was, how the soldiers were and how the war was going. ⁸Then David said to Uriah, "Go down to your house and wash your feet." So Uriah left the palace, and a gift from the king was sent after him. ⁹But Uriah slept at the entrance to the palace with all his master's servants and did not go down to his house.
¹⁰When David was told, "Uriah did not go home," he asked him, "Haven't you just come from a distance? Why didn't you go home?"

[11]Uriah said to David, "The ark and Israel and Judah are staying in tents, and my master Joab and my lord's men are camped in the open fields. How could I go to my house to eat and drink and lie with my wife? As surely as you live, I will not do such a thing!"

[12]Then David said to him, "Stay here one more day, and tomorrow I will send you back." So Uriah remained in Jerusalem that day and the next. [13]At David's invitation, he ate and drank with him, and David made him drunk. But in the evening Uriah went out to sleep on his mat among his master's servants; he did not go home.

[14]In the morning David wrote a letter to Joab and sent it with Uriah. [15]In it he wrote, "Put Uriah in the front line where the fighting is fiercest. Then withdraw from him so he will be struck down and die."

[16]So while Joab had the city under siege, he put Uriah at a place where he knew the strongest defenders were. [17]When the men of the city came out and fought against Joab, some of the men in David's army fell; moreover, Uriah the Hittite died.

[26]When Uriah's wife heard that her husband was dead, she mourned for him. [27]After the time of mourning was over, David had her brought to his house, and she became his wife and bore him a son. But the thing David had done displeased the Lord.

Was David's choice right or wrong?
❏ Right ❏ Wrong Why? _____

Did David try to justify his choice to become physically involved with Bathsheba? ❏ Yes ❏ No

What reasons could he have given to make his conduct seem "right?"

_____

_____

Did David try to judge right and wrong by his passions?
❏ Yes ❏ No

Does the scriptural account give any indication that David considered the choice? ❏ Yes ❏ No

If yes, circle or underline a verse or portion of a verse from 2 Samuel 11 to illustrate your answer.

Did David consider the choice at that moment as a choice between what was objectively right and what was objectively wrong—regardless of what he thought or felt?   ❑ Yes   ❑ No

Look Inside

What about you? Do you ever try to judge right and wrong by your passions?   ❑ Yes   ❑ No

If your answer was yes, in what situations are you most likely to try to judge right and wrong by your passions?

_____

_____

Do you think children and youth ever notice how your passions affect your judgment in those situations?   ❑ Yes   ❑ No

If so, what can you do to consider the choice, to start making your choices based on a belief in an objective, universal, constant standard of right and wrong? By doing so, you will set a new, different example for others.

_____

_____

Spend a few moments in prayer, using the following as a guide.
- Praise God because He is righteous, loving, holy, and true.
- Talk to God honestly about the changes you would like to make in the way you make choices, and the changes you would like to see in the way children and youth make choices.
- Ask God to give you patience and perseverance as you continue this study.
- Pray for your family and friends, asking God to use you to influence and bless them.

Compare It to God

DAY THREE

A sleepy Jean wrestled into her Sunday clothes and shuffled back into the bathroom. The mirror was still fogged from the hot shower she had taken a few moments before.

She snatched a hand towel from the rack and wiped the mirror, clearing a space large enough for her to put her contact lenses in her still-sleepy eyes.

Jim had left a little before midnight last night. Their passion had carried them further than ever before, but they had stayed true to their determination not to go "all the way."

Jean looked unsmilingly at her reflection. "I don't feel guilty," she whispered, as if trying to convince herself. "Why should I? I love him and he loves me, that's all that matters."

She stared at herself, unmoving. The mirror began to fog again, and she reached for the towel.

The bathroom mirror isn't the only thing that keeps fogging up for Jean. Her thinking isn't too clear, either, because she's trying to judge the rightness or wrongness of her actions. She's not considering the choice as a choice between what is right or wrong objectively regardless of what she thinks. Consequently, she's not proceeding to the next step in the 4Cs process, which is: _____

Dare to Compare

Realistically, Jean may be reluctant to submit her decision to the 4Cs process because she doesn't want to compare her actions to the nature and character of God. Jean may be afraid of what she'll discover.

What would she discover if she were to compare her action to God? What would she learn by tracing her action (through precept and principle) to the Person of God Himself?

Precept • In biblical terms, sexual immorality is all extramarital sex. God has spoken through the law, and He has made His standard clear: all sexual involvement outside of marriage is wrong.

Paraphrase the precept as it is expressed in the following verses.

You are to abstain from food sacrificed to idols, from blood, from the meat of strangled animals and from sexual immorality. You will do well to avoid these things (Acts 15:29).

_____

Flee from sexual immorality. All other sins a man commits are outside his body, but he who sins sexually sins against his own body (1 Corinthians 6:18).

_____

We should not commit sexual immorality, as some of them did—and in one day twenty-three thousand of them died (1 Corinthians 10:8).

_____

But among you there must not be even a hint of sexual immorality, or of greed, because these are improper for God's holy people (Ephesians 5:3).

_____

Put to death, therefore, whatever belongs to your earthly nature: sexual immorality, impurity, lust, evil desires and greed, which is idolatry (Colossians 3:5).

_____

It is God's will that you should be holy; that you should avoid sexual immorality (1 Thessalonians 4:3).

_____

Do these precepts apply to Jim and Jean's situation?

❏ Yes, because _____

_____

❏ No, because _____

_____

Principle • What positive principle or principles do you think lie behind those precepts?

_____

The biblical commands to "flee sexual immorality" are based on God's standards for sex, which actually incorporate three principles: love, purity, and faithfulness.

According to the verses below, true love is evident when the happiness, health, and spiritual growth of another person is as important to you as your own.

> ⁹The commandments, "Do not commit adultery," "Do not murder," "Do not steal," "Do not covet," and whatever other commandment there may be, are summed up in this one rule: "Love your neighbor as yourself." ¹⁰Love does no harm to its neighbor. Therefore love is the fulfillment of the law (Romans 13:9-10).

> In this same way, husbands ought to love their wives as their own bodies. He who loves his wife loves himself (Ephesians 5:28)

God's standard for sex is one of purity. Circle the two words in Hebrews 13:4 that indicate God's desire for marriage and the marriage bed.

> Marriage should be honored by all, and the marriage bed kept pure, for God will judge the adulterer and all the sexually immoral.

God designed sex to be enjoyed in a husband-wife relationship for procreation (Genesis 1:28), for spiritual unity (Genesis 2:24), and for pleasure (Proverbs 5:18-19). Sexual bonding is meant to form an unbroken circle, a pure union: two virgins entering an exclusive relationship. That circle, that union, can be broken even *before* marriage, if one or both of the partners has not remained pure by waiting to have sex until it can be experienced in the purity of a husband-wife relationship.

God's standard for sex is also one of faithfulness. Love "always protects, always trusts, always hopes, always perseveres" (1 Corinthians 13:7). "Love and faithfulness meet together" (Psalm 85:10). In practical terms, this means that true love requires a commitment of two people to remain faithful to each other. That is why marriage is central to biblical sexuality, because it binds two people together in a lifelong commitment. If love is to produce the emotional, physical, and spiritual intimacy it is designed to produce, it must be committed, faithful love. Jim and Jean may be talking about marriage, they might even get engaged, but until they are husband and wife, they have not fully committed to each other and fulfilled God's requirement for sex.

God's precepts regarding human sexuality are grounded upon the principles of love, purity, and faithfulness. Those principles, in turn, reflect the person of God Himself.

Person • The principles of love, purity, and faithfulness are right because they are from God—they reflect His nature and character. Read the following Bible verses, and complete the statement that follows each verse.

> Whoever does not love does not know God, because God is love (1 John 4:8).

God is _____

> Everyone who has this hope in him purifies himself, just as he is pure (1 John 3:3).

God is _____

> Know therefore that the Lord your God is God; he is the faithful God, keeping his covenant of love to a thousand generations of those who love him and keep his commands (Deuteronomy 7:9).

God is the _____ God.

Jim and Jean need to compare their sexual activity to the nature and character of God (instead of justifying it by their passions). Help them determine whether the following statements are true or false by circling *T* for True, *F* for False.

T F Our action is loving; it promotes the happiness, health, and spiritual growth of the other person.

T F Our action is pure; it does not defile the marriage bed by permitting activity that should be reserved for a husband or wife.

T F Our action is faithful; both partners have made a lifetime commitment of marriage.

Shine the Light

Because God is pure, sexual impurity is an offense against Him. Because God is faithful, sex outside of a marriage commitment is an affront to Him. King David, who sinned with Bathsheba, later repented; he confessed to God, "Against you, you only, have I sinned and done what is evil in your sight" (Psalm 51:4). Was David ignoring the fact that his sin had affected other people, resulting in the death of Bathsheba's husband, Uriah, and of the baby Bathsheba bore David? No, David was acknowledging the fundamental fact that when he sinned with Bathsheba, he sinned against the Lawgiver. His act was wrong because it offended God's standard for sex: love, purity, and faithfulness.

Do your relationships conform to God's standard?
- If you are married, will you make a commitment to God and your mate to marital faithfulness in thought and deed? ❏ Yes ❏ No
- If you are single, will you make a commitment to God to remain sexually abstinent until the day you enter a biblical marriage relationship? ❏ Yes ❏ No

Are you setting an example for children and youth, based on an objective, constant, and universal standard? Or are you tolerating wrong attitudes or actions in this area? If your actions do not conform to God's standard in this area, turn to David's prayer in Psalm 51 as we presented it on pages 111-112. Pray the prayer again.

Close your study time today by asking God to make your relationships (present and/or future) loving, faithful, and pure. Then ask God to help you guide children and youth into relationships that reflect His nature, too.

DAY FOUR

Commit to God's Way

Jim sat in the choir loft at church, his choir folder open on his lap. The choir director lifted her arms as the pastor concluded his sermon.

Jim opened his mouth to sing, but nothing came out; instead, he watched with wide-eyed interest as Jean rose from her seat in the congregation and walked forward to kneel at the front of the sanctuary.

He watched his girlfriend, thoughts racing through his head like hockey players skating back and forth in a hockey rink.

What's she doing? he wondered. *I hope she's not having second thoughts about last night. I hope she's not feeling guilty, like we did something wrong.*

He stared at her intensely, as if he could transmit his will to her by sheer willpower. *Don't let it bother you, Jean. We're too much in love.*

The choir sang all around Jim, but he never even looked in the choir director's direction.

You've got nothing to repent for, he told Jean, who still knelt alone. *Don't ruin it all now. Don't ruin it all.*

Jim is in trouble. He has not entirely convinced himself that his activity with Jean is perfectly OK. He senses that, if he did consider the choice and compare it to God, he and Jean would have to admit the wrongness of their actions. So, Jim's stubbornly trying to ignore what his heart and mind know—that he should turn from his own selfish ways and commit to God's way.

Better Late Than Never

Jim's not the first to make that mistake. Perhaps you have made the same mistake.

Remember King David and his bad choices with Bathsheba? You probably know that the story didn't end after David engineered the death of Uriah, Bathsheba's husband.

Read 2 Samuel 12:1-13 on the following page.

¹The LORD sent Nathan to David. When he came to him, he said, "There were two men in a certain town, one rich and the other poor. ²The rich man had a very large number of sheep and cattle, ³but the poor man had nothing except one little ewe lamb he had bought. He raised it, and it grew up with him and his children. It shared his food, drank from his cup and even slept in his arms. It was like a daughter to him.

⁴"Now a traveler came to the rich man, but the rich man refrained from taking one of his own sheep or cattle to prepare a meal for the traveler who had come to him. Instead, he took the ewe lamb that belonged to the poor man and prepared it for the one who had come to him."

⁵David burned with anger against the man and said to Nathan, "As surely as the LORD lives, the man who did this deserves to die! ⁶He must pay for that lamb four times over, because he did such a thing and had no pity."

⁷Then Nathan said to David, "You are the man! This is what the LORD, the God of Israel, says: 'I anointed you king over Israel, and I delivered you from the hand of Saul. ⁸I gave your master's house to you, and your master's wives into your arms. I gave you the house of Israel and Judah. And if all this had been too little, I would have given you even more. ⁹Why did you despise the word of the LORD by doing what is evil in his eyes? You struck down Uriah the Hittite with the sword and took his wife to be your own. You killed him with the sword of the Ammonites. ¹⁰Now, therefore, the sword will never depart from your house, because you despised me and took the wife of Uriah the Hittite to be your own.'

¹¹"This is what the LORD says: 'Out of your own household I am going to bring calamity upon you. Before your very eyes I will take your wives and give them to one who is close to you, and he will lie with your wives in broad daylight. ¹²You did it in secret, but I will do this thing in broad daylight before all Israel.' "

¹³Then David said to Nathan, "I have sinned against the LORD."

Nathan replied, "The LORD has taken away your sin. You are not going to die."

How did David finally come to admit that his actions were wrong?
- ❑ The Lord used Nathan to guide David to see the wrong in what he had done.
- ❑ Bathsheba confronted David.
- ❑ David prayed to God and God convicted David of his sins.

Does verse 13 reflect a sudden realization or did David sense his sinfulness all along? ❏ Yes ❏ No Why or why not?

_____

_____

Which of the 4Cs corresponds with verse 13? Check the one that applies.
   ❏ Consider the choice.
   ❏ Compare it to God.
   ❏ Commit to God's way.
   ❏ Count on God's protection and provision.

Read Psalm 51:1-17, the song David composed after the prophet Nathan confronted him with his sin.

Have mercy on me, O God,
   according to your unfailing love;
   according to your great compassion
   blot out my transgressions.
Wash away all my iniquity
   and cleanse me from my sin.

For I know my transgressions,
   and my sin is always before me.
Against you, you only, have I sinned
   and done what is evil in your sight,
   so that you are proved right when you speak
   and justified when you judge.
Surely I was sinful at birth,
   sinful from the time my mother conceived me.
Surely you desire truth in the inner parts;
   you teach me wisdom
   in the inmost place.

Cleanse me with hyssop, and I will be clean;
   wash me, and I will be whiter than snow.
Let me hear joy and gladness;
   let the bones you have crushed rejoice.
Hide your face from my sins
   and blot out all my iniquity.

Create in me a pure heart, O God,
   and renew a steadfast spirit within me.
Do not cast me from your presence
   or take your Holy Spirit from me.
Restore to me the joy of your salvation
   and grant me a willing spirit, to sustain me.

Then I will teach transgressors your ways,
    and sinners will turn back to you.
Save me from bloodguilt, O God,
    the God who saves me,
    and my tongue will sing of your righteousness.
O Lord, open my lips,
    and my mouth will declare your praise.
You do not delight in sacrifice, or I would bring it;
    you do not take pleasure in burnt offerings.
The sacrifices of God are a
    broken spirit;
    a broken and contrite heart,
    O God, you will not despise.

Based on these verses, do you think David committed to God's way? ❏ Yes ❏ No Why or why not?

_____

_____

Write in the margin Colossians 3:5. Say it aloud three times.

Better Safe Than Sorry

How is David's situation similar to Jim and Jean's? _____

_____

_____

How is it different? _____

_____

_____

What would committing to God's way involve for Jim? Check all that apply. The list continues on the next page.
    ❏ Break up with Jean.
    ❏ Keep his mouth shut and see what happens.
    ❏ Admit his sexual sin to God.
    ❏ Marry Jean immediately.
    ❏ Join the circus.
    ❏ Determine to save all forms of sexual intimacy for marriage.
    ❏ "Go all the way" with Jean.
    ❏ Resolve to build a relationship that reflects love, purity, and faithfulness.
    ❏ Become a monk.

❑ Focus on the spiritual, emotional, and intellectual parts of their relationship while steering away from physical intimacy.
❑ Avoid being alone with Jean in dark or secluded places.
❑ Avoid being alone with anybody in dark or secluded places.
❑ Avoid dark or secluded places.

Would committing to God's way would be easy for Jim?
❑ Yes ❑ No

What do you think would be most difficult for him? _____

_____

What is difficult for you about committing to God's way in this area?

_____

Can you give that problem to God? ❑ Yes ❑ No

Why or why not? _____

_____

Close today's study by writing your own "Psalm 51" below in which you admit God's sovereignty, submit to His version of what's right or wrong, and commit to following His ways in the power of His Holy Spirit.

_____

_____

_____

_____

_____

Count on God's Protection and Provision

Jim gripped Jean by the elbow and pulled her aside in the church foyer.

"Are you OK?" he asked, his eyes searching her face for clues as to why she had knelt in the front of the sanctuary at the end of the morning service.

"Yeah," she nodded, avoiding his gaze. "We need to talk."

Jim didn't like the sound of that. "Walk you out to the parking lot?" he suggested.

Jean nodded. She folded her arms, and they walked in silence to a corner of the church parking lot. They paused by a sprawling six-foot juniper bush.

"What's up?" he asked, fearing he already knew the answer.

She looked into Jim's brown eyes and swallowed hard. Then she dropped her gaze to the ground. "I prayed about last night," she whispered. "I told God I knew it was wrong, and I told Him I'd try not to do it again."

"What did we do?" Jim asked, his voice rising suddenly in pitch. "We didn't do anything!"

She didn't answer, but her expression clearly communicated that she knew better.

"Look," Jim said, consciously controlling his voice, "I love you. And I thought you loved me."

"I do."

"If this is about getting engaged—"

"No," she answered calmly. "It's not. It's about doing what's right." He started to interrupt, but she wouldn't let him. "Not what you say is right, and not what I say is right. It's about what God says."

"So," Jim said slowly, pausing between words. "What about us?

We're still a couple, right?"

She looked at him without blinking. "I don't know," she said. "I don't know."

Can You Count?

Did Jean …
- ❏ make the right decision?
- ❏ make a big mistake?

What were the immediate results of her choice? List them below.

_____

_____

_____

Are the results immediately positive or negative?

❏ Positive, because _____

_____

❏ Negative, because _____

_____

The last of the 4Cs, you'll remember, is to count on God's protection and provision. What kinds of protection and provision do you think could result from Jean's decision to commit to God's way?

Protection: _____

_____

Provision: _____

_____

Jean may have made her decision based on these potential benefits; she also made her decision based on her obedience to God. Trusting Him with the results, she is paving the way for a much happier, healthier future. Why?

• *God's standards for sexual behavior protect from guilt.* God defines right and wrong. When we transgress His standards, we will invariably suffer guilt. Jean and Jim's repeated assertions that they had no reason to feel guilty should have tipped them off; they felt it necessary to convince themselves because they did feel guilty.

• *God's standards for sexual behavior also provide spiritual rewards.* The blessing of a clear conscience and an unhindered walk with God are inestimable. It is an immeasurable blessing to be able to stand before an altar and proclaim the singular devotion of your body to your mate and to God. The sexual relationship between a husband and wife is not only pleasurable, it is sacred.

• *God's standards for sexual behavior protect from unplanned pregnancies and abortions.* Every day in America, 2,795 teenage girls get pregnant and 1,106 have an abortion. Those girls who carry their babies for the full term often face overwhelming difficulties. Many drop out of school, many experience physical problems, many feel left out of "normal" teen activities because of their responsibility to a child. Those girls who abort their children are not delivered from such consequences; abortion produces traumatic results, too. Over half report preoccupation with the aborted child, flashbacks of the abortion experience, and nightmares related to the abortion.[1]

• *God's standards for sexual behavior protect from sexually transmitted diseases.* Every day in America, 4,219 teenagers contract a sexually transmitted disease. Yet *not one* of those incidents has occurred between two mutually faithful partners who entered the relationship sexually pure ... because God's standards for sexual behavior protect from diseases.

• *God's standards for sexual behavior provide for peace of mind.* Two people who adhere to God's wise model will enjoy a relationship free of fear, free of disease, free of the "ghosts" of past partners, and free of "emotional baggage" as a result of a past immoral relationship.

• *God's standards for sexual behavior provide for trust.* Sexual purity and faithfulness before marriage contributes to an atmosphere of trust within marriage. That trust provides peace of mind for both partners when they are apart; each knows that the other is worthy of trust. Why? Because, in the period before their marriage, they proved their character, their maturity, and their self-control.

• *God's standards for sexual behavior provide for true intimacy.* God's standard for sexual behavior produces a degree of intimacy that only exists in the committed exclusivity of a marriage relationship. "For this reason," God said, "a man will leave his father and mother and be united to his wife, and they will become one flesh" (Genesis 2:24).

God's design for sexual intimacy protects from many dangers and provides the best climate for the enjoyment of spiritual rewards, peace of mind, trust, intimacy, and many other benefits to be enjoyed in a lifelong relationship of purity and faithfulness.

Costly Choice

The story of David and Bathsheba graphically depicts the results of David's refusal to follow God's way. Read 2 Samuel 12:13-25.

[13]Then David said to Nathan, "I have sinned against the LORD."

Nathan replied, "The LORD has taken away your sin. You are not going to die. [14]But because by doing this you have made the enemies of the LORD show utter contempt, the son born to you will die."

[15]After Nathan had gone home, the LORD struck the child that Uriah's wife had borne to David, and he became ill. [16]David pleaded with God for the child. He fasted and went into his house and spent the nights lying on the ground. [17]The elders of his household stood beside him to get him up from the ground, but he refused, and he would not eat any food with them.

[18]On the seventh day the child died. David's servants were afraid to tell him that the child was dead, for they thought, "While the child was still living, we spoke to David but he would not listen to us. How can we tell him the child is dead? He may do something desperate."

[19]David noticed that his servants were whispering among themselves and he realized the child was dead. "Is the child dead?" he asked.

"Yes," they replied, "he is dead."

[20]Then David got up from the ground. After he had washed, put on lotions and changed his clothes, he went into the house of the Lord and worshiped. Then he went to his own house, and at his request they served him food, and he ate.

[21]His servants asked him, "Why are you acting this way? While the child was alive, you fasted and wept, but now that the child is dead, you get up and eat!"

[22]He answered, "While the child was still alive, I fasted and wept. I thought, 'Who knows? The LORD may be gracious to me and let the child live.' [23]But now that he is dead, why should I fast? Can I bring him back again? I will go to him, but he will not return to me."

[24]Then David comforted his wife Bathsheba, and he went to her and lay with her. She gave birth to a son, and they named him Solomon. The LORD loved him; [25]and because the Lord loved him, he sent word through Nathan the prophet to name him Jedidiah.

Answer the following questions about David and Bathsheba by circling the correct answer. Answers are provided at the end of today's study.

1. As a result of David's choice, Bathsheba became:
   a. pregnant.
   b. David's wife.
   c. a widow.
   d. all of the above.
2. As a result of David's choice, God:
   a. stopped loving David.
   b. rewarded David.
   c. was displeased with David.
   d. struck David with leprosy.
3. As a result of David's choice, the baby:
   a. grew up to be king.
   b. became a great warrior.
   c. brought years of joy to his parents.
   d. none of the above.
4. As a result of David's choice, David:
   a. brought shame on the name of the Lord.
   b. lost his firstborn son.
   c. spent seven days in agony and uncertainty.
   d. all of the above.

Looking back on his sin with Bathsheba, did David experience immediate benefits as a result of his decision? ❏ Yes ❏ No

Were the above consequences worth the immediate benefits?
❏ Yes ❏ No Why or why not?

_____

Would a young person answer the above question differently?
❏ Yes ❏ No Why or why not?

_____

_____

What can you do to convince or reinforce in children and youth a recognition that obeying God and counting on his long-term protection and provision (like Jean) is a wiser and happier choice than choosing wrong in order to get immediate benefits (like David)?

_____

_____

Close today's study in prayer, using the following as a guide.

> *Father, I praise You because You are a loving and right-eous God. Thank You for Your desire to protect me and provide for Your children. I sincerely want to please You and enjoy the blessings of following Your ways. I want the children and youth in my life, [mention them by name] to do the same. Give me wisdom and courage to guide them through what I do and say.*
> *As I face important choices, help me to:*
>   *Consider the choice,*
>   *Compare it to You,*
>   *Commit to Your way, and then*
>   *Count on Your protection and provision.*
>
> *I trust You to help me do that every day by Your Holy Spirit, and to help me, by word and deed, to influence others. In Jesus' name, amen.*

Answers to costly choice exercise: 1., d.; 2., c.; 3., d.; 4., d.

[1]Anne Catherine Speckhard, "Psycho-Social Aspects of Stress Following Abortion" (doctoral dissertation, University of Minnesota, 1985), n.p.

I learned that _____

_____

_____

One attitude I had which changed was _____

_____

_____

God spoke to me by _____

_____

_____

One behavior that I will examine is _____

_____

_____

When I shared with the child or youth in my life, _____

_____

_____

The most difficult thing was _____

_____

_____

It was a joy to _____

_____

_____

Tomorrow I will _____

_____

_____

My Scripture memory verse is_____

_____

WEEKLY JOURNAL

WEEK SEVEN

The Stand

No one did it better than Joe Montana. Montana, who played quarterback for football's San Francisco 49ers and, later, for the Kansas City Chiefs, produced results when faced with a seemingly impossible challenge. Time after time throughout his long career, Montana would take the field with his team trailing on the scoreboard and a mere two minutes of playing time on the clock. Time after time, he engineered a last-second score that won the game.

Some players seem to enter the last two minutes of a football game with the thought, "It's almost over." Joe Montana responded to the two-minute warning with the attitude, "The real excitement's just begun."

For the past six weeks, you've been on a journey of discovery, learning about the crisis of truth that threatens today's children and youth. You've reasoned through many issues regarding right and wrong. You've discovered the 4Cs process for discerning and choosing right, and applied it to issues such as honesty, love, and sex. You've searched the Scriptures and come to understand that the line between right and wrong is a reflection of God's nature and character; what is like God is right, and what is unlike God is wrong.

Today you begin the last week of study in *Truth Matters*. If you've worked diligently through the past six weeks of studies and participated in the group sessions, you should have a good understanding of absolute truth, how to discern it, and how to follow it.

But you're not finished yet. You might say this is the two-minute warning. The game's not over. This is no time to let up; if anything, it's time to play with more intensity and determination than before.

This week you will—
- encounter the "three pillars" that will help you effectively communicate truth to children and youth;
- devise strategies to implement the three pillars;
- prepare for the opposition you may face when you begin to "tell the truth" beyond your immediate family or church family; and
- plan the next steps you and your church can take to reflect your conviction that truth matters.

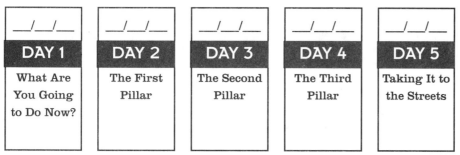

__/__/__	__/__/__	__/__/__	__/__/__	__/__/__
DAY 1	**DAY 2**	**DAY 3**	**DAY 4**	**DAY 5**
What Are You Going to Do Now?	The First Pillar	The Second Pillar	The Third Pillar	Taking It to the Streets

(Add the day/month/year to indicate when you complete your study.)

A key passage to memorize

These commandments that I give you today are to be upon your hearts. Impress them on your children. Talk about them when you sit at home and when you walk along the road, when you lie down and when you get up (Deuteronomy 6:6-7).

Concepts you will come to understand

- The three pillars of "truth-telling"
- Truth and tolerance

This Week's Assignments

- Memorize Deuteronomy 6:6-7.
- Complete daily exercises.
- Ask your child or teenager (and brace yourself for the answer!), "Do I act like someone who believes that some things are definitely right and some things are definitely wrong? Do I always model God's truth the way I should?" Try to be open and honest with your children and youth, and ask them to suggest ways you might become a more effective model of God's truth.
- Give the children and youth permission to remind you of the 4Cs when you face a decision. You may be surprised how that will motivate them to apply the 4Cs!
- Continue to be open to teaching moments. It's more effective to have many, brief, to-the-point interactions with a young person instead of a few long lectures. Consult the book *Right From Wrong* for more suggestions for teaching the truth to the children and youth in your life.
- Complete your Weekly Journal.

DAY ONE

What Are You Going to Do Now?

You've seen the commercials.

A winning quarterback is running off the football field. He stops to grin at the camera. An off-camera voice calls him by name and asks, "You've just won the Super Bowl; what are you going to do now?"

A tennis pro serves the winning ace and pumps her arms victoriously in the air. As she walks off the court, an off-camera voice calls her by name and says, "You've just won Wimbledon; what are you going to do now?"

The answer in each case, of course, is: "I'm going to Disney World!"

Suppose you're in a commercial right now. Two reporters approach you. One points a big video camera at you, and the other shoves a microphone in your face. The one with the microphone calls you by name and says, "You've just learned Who determines right and wrong, how to discern what's right, and how to do right. What are you going to do now?"

How would you answer? _____

_____

The Next Step

Of course, you're not the first to make new and sometimes startling discoveries about truth. Others have done so before you. Let's look at what they did upon learning the truth. Perhaps their example is one you can follow.

Read the following accounts of various individuals who encountered the truth. Complete the question following the name and the reference, and write how you think that person would have answered the question, "What are you going to do now?"

> [14]While they were bringing out the money that had been taken into the temple of the LORD, Hilkiah the priest found the Book of the Law of the LORD that had been given

through Moses. ¹⁵Hilkiah said to Shaphan the secretary, "I have found the Book of the Law in the temple of the LORD." He gave it to Shaphan.

¹⁶Then Shaphan took the book to the king and reported to him: "Your officials are doing everything that has been committed to them. ¹⁷They have paid out the money that was in the temple of the LORD and have entrusted it to the supervisors and workers." ¹⁸Then Shaphan the secretary informed the king, "Hilkiah the priest has given me a book." And Shaphan read from it in the presence of the king.

¹⁹When the king heard the words of the Law, he tore his robes.

²⁹Then the king called together all the elders of Judah and Jerusalem. ³⁰He went up to the temple of the LORD with the men of Judah, the people of Jerusalem, the priests and the Levites—all the people from the least to the greatest. He read in their hearing all the words of the Book of the Covenant, which had been found in the temple of the LORD. ³¹The king stood by his pillar and renewed the covenant in the presence of the LORD—to follow the LORD and keep his commands, regulations and decrees with all his heart and all his soul, and to obey the words of the covenant written in this book.

³²Then he had everyone in Jerusalem and Benjamin pledge themselves to it; the people of Jerusalem did this in accordance with the covenant of God, the God of their fathers (2 Chronicles 34:14-19, 29-32).

"Josiah, king of Judah, you've just _____

What are you going to do now?" _____

_____

¹King Belshazzar gave a great banquet for a thousand of his nobles and drank wine with them. ²While Belshazzar was drinking his wine, he gave orders to bring in the gold and silver goblets that Nebuchadnezzar his father had taken from the temple in Jerusalem, so that the king and his nobles, his wives and his concubines might drink from them. ³So they brought in the gold goblets that had been taken from the temple of God in Jerusalem, and the king and his nobles, his wives and his concubines drank from them. ⁴As they drank the wine, they praised the gods of gold and silver, of bronze, iron, wood and stone.

⁵Suddenly the fingers of a human hand appeared and wrote on the plaster of the wall, near the lampstand in the royal palace. The king watched the hand as it wrote. ⁶His

face turned pale and he was so frightened that his knees knocked together and his legs gave way.

¹³So Daniel was brought before the king, and the king said to him, "Are you Daniel, one of the exiles my father the king brought from Judah? ¹⁴I have heard that the spirit of the gods is in you and that you have insight, intelligence and outstanding wisdom. ¹⁵The wise men and enchanters were brought before me to read this writing and tell me what it means, but they could not explain it. ¹⁶Now I have heard that you are able to give interpretations and to solve difficult problems. If you can read this writing and tell me what it means, you will be clothed in purple and have a gold chain placed around your neck, and you will be made the third highest ruler in the kingdom."

¹⁷Then Daniel answered the king, "You may keep your gifts for yourself and give your rewards to someone else. Nevertheless, I will read the writing for the king and tell him what it means (Daniel 5:1-6, 13-17).

"Daniel, you've just _____

What are you going to do now?"_____

⁴³The next day Jesus decided to leave for Galilee. Finding Philip, he said to him, "Follow me."

⁴⁴Philip, like Andrew and Peter, was from the town of Bethsaida. ⁴⁵Philip found Nathanael and told him, "We have found the one Moses wrote about in the Law, and about whom the prophets also wrote—Jesus of Nazareth, the son of Joseph."

⁴⁶"Nazareth! Can anything good come from there?" Nathanael asked.

"Come and see," said Philip (John 1:43-46).

"Philip of Bethsaida, you've just _____

What are you going to do now?"_____

¹⁰Then the disciples went back to their homes, ¹¹but Mary stood outside the tomb crying. As she wept, she bent over to look into the tomb ¹²and saw two angels in white, seated where Jesus' body had been, one at the head and the other at the foot.

¹³They asked her, "Woman, why are you crying?"

"They have taken my Lord away," she said, "and I don't know where they have put him." ¹⁴At this, she turned around and saw Jesus standing there, but she did not realize that it was Jesus.

[15]"Woman," he said, "why are you crying? Who is it you are looking for?"

Thinking he was the gardener, she said, "Sir, if you have carried him away, tell me where you have put him, and I will get him."

[16]Jesus said to her, "Mary."

She turned toward him and cried out in Aramaic, "Rabboni!" (which means Teacher).

[17]Jesus said, "Do not hold on to me, for I have not yet returned to the Father. Go instead to my brothers and tell them, 'I am returning to my Father and your Father, to my God and your God.' "

[18]Mary Magdalene went to the disciples with the news: "I have seen the Lord!" And she told them that he had said these things to her (John 20:10-18).

"Mary Magdalene, you've just _____

What are you going to do now?"_____

_____

What did each of those individuals do upon obtaining new insight into the truth?

_____

To Tell the Truth

If we learn how to make the right choices when we're faced with moral decisions, we possess a priceless knowledge. And that very knowledge carries a profound responsibility. First Timothy 2:3-4 makes God's will very clear. According to those verses, what does God want? Circle your answer in the following verses.

[3]This is good, and pleases God our Savior, [4]who wants all men to be saved and to come to a knowledge of the truth.

Because you know the truth, God's call to you is to *tell* the truth. To return to the football terminology we used in the introduction, God wants you to hand off the ball to someone else, and He wants you to do it in a timely manner and without a costly fumble.

Of course, that's not always easy; but there are ways to increase your chances of making the transfer of truth. We'll discuss these ways in tomorrow's study.

Look at 1 Timothy 2:3-4 again. Based on this passage, respond honestly to the statements below, checking all that apply, to help you gauge how you're responding to today's study.

	Agree	Disagree	Don't Know
I feel like it's too late; my kids are too old.	❏	❏	❏
I feel like I've got to get my life "ironed out" before I can help anyone else to a knowledge of the truth.	❏	❏	❏
I don't think I know enough Scripture to communicate the truth effectively.	❏	❏	❏
I don't know how to tell others what I've discovered about the truth.	❏	❏	❏
I'm afraid my relationship with the children and youth in my life has deteriorated too badly to begin teaching right from wrong now.	❏	❏	❏
I think kids have to figure out such things for themselves.	❏	❏	❏
I'm afraid no one will listen to me.	❏	❏	❏
I feel like I'd be a hypocrite if I try to teach the truth when I didn't make right choices when I was younger.	❏	❏	❏

This week's study will address some of the above concerns or difficulties, but take a moment right now to bow before God in prayer and discuss the above responses with Him. Remember that your emotions and your will are not the same, so be honest about your feelings (the response of your emotions) while also committing to God's way (the response of your will).

The First Pillar

Communicating a cohesive model of truth and objective morality to your children, students, or youth group may seem nearly impossible. Not only do we have to bring abstract concepts into the "real, relevant, right now" world of young people, but it seems like a never-ending process. That's because it *is* never-ending. The responsibility of adults seems daunting partly because it is constant. But it is the constant, consistent element of our teaching that will instill truth in the next generation.

The Three Pillars

Picture a structure in the classical Greek style, a foundation ringed by several steps that lead to a columned building. Now imagine that the steps represent the steps to truth that you've discovered in this study. Those steps lead individuals into the structure itself, which is supported by three pillars. Each of the pillars is necessary, of course; the strength of each contributes to the effectiveness of them all. These three pillars symbolize relationship, example, and truth.

Keep that picture in mind as we discuss the three pillars that will help you communicate biblical truth to your children, grandchildren, students, youth group, or friends.

Build a Relationship

The first pillar of effective communication is relationship. That's what biblical morality is all about: our relationships with God and with others. We cannot impart truth, therefore, apart from honest, meaningful relationships.

Simply occupying a position of authority, such as pastor, teacher, youth minister or leader, coach, mother, or father by no means guarantees that you can effectively teach a young person right from wrong. Anyone who wishes to pass on biblical values to someone else must begin by developing a strong, positive relationship with that person, because truth is best understood in the context of a relationship.

God gave Israel the model for teaching truth to children and youth in Deuteronomy 6:4-9. This passage contains our memory passage for the week. Read the verses below and fill in the missing words or phrases indicated by the blanks.

⁴"Hear, O Israel: The LORD our God, the LORD is one. ⁵Love the LORD your God with all your heart and with all your

soul and with all your strength. These commandments that I give you today, shall be _____.
⁷Impress them on your children. Talk about them when you _____ and when you _____, when you _____ and when you _____. ⁸Tie them as symbols on your hands and bind them on your foreheads. ⁹Write them on the door-frames of your houses and on your gates" (Deuteronomy 6:4-9).

Repeat the passage aloud three times. These verses are a good reminder of our responsibility to pass along to children and youth God's standard of right and wrong.

God's model for teaching truth to children and youth called not only for a constant process but also prescribed a relational method as well.

How do you determine the depth and breadth of your relationship with a child or teenager? Answer the following questions as completely and accurately as possible for each of the young people you most wish to influence.

When is the last time you laughed together? _____

_____

When is the last time you cried together? _____

_____

Do you know what his favorite (current) song is? _____

_____

Do you know who she sits with in the school cafeteria? _____

_____

When did he last seek your advice? _____

_____

When did you last forget or cancel a commitment to her?

_____

Do you more often ask questions of or make statements to him?

_____

Have you recently admitted a mistake or fault to her? _____

_____

What do you really know about his spiritual life? _____

_____

The answers to such questions are not exhaustive, of course, but they may help you gauge the depth of your relationships. They may also suggest places to start deepening them right now.

Starting Now

Regardless of the ages of your children or youth (or those young people you most wish to influence), it is never too late to build relationships.

> I recall a Portland woman whose four adult children had completely rebelled against her and caused her untold agonies and heartaches. Dick Day [my friend and co-author] and I shared the relationship-building principles from [our book] *How to Be a Hero to your Kids*, and she went home committed to the long, hard task of rebuilding those relationships. Five years later, we met that woman again. She said that her relationship with two of her children had turned around 180 degrees! She shared tearfully how attention to relationship—even with adult children—had paid rich dividends (*Right From Wrong*, 125).

In what areas do you feel the most need for improvement in your relationship(s) with the children and youth you want to influence?

_____

_____

What are the four most important things you can do now to begin improving your relationship(s) with the significant children and youth in your life? Possibilities include activities such as Reading a bedtime story at least four nights a week, Learning to play the video games Jason likes so much, Taking Angela out on a 'date' once a month, Eating dinner at the table instead of in front of the TV. Now write yours on the next page.

1. _____

2. _____

3. _____

4. _____

Read Ephesians 3:14-21 below.

> [14]For this reason I kneel before the Father, [15]from whom his whole family in heaven and on earth derives its name. [16]I pray that out of his glorious riches he may strengthen you with power through his Spirit in your inner being, [17]so that Christ may dwell in your hearts through faith. And I pray that you, being rooted and established in love, [18]may have power, together with all the saints, to grasp how wide and long and high and deep is the love of Christ, [19]and to know this love that surpasses knowledge—that you may be filled to the measure of all the fullness of God.
>
> [20]Now to him who is able to do immeasurably more than all we ask or imagine, according to his power that is at work within us, [21]to him be glory in the church and in Christ Jesus throughout all generations, for ever and ever! Amen.

Direct these words to God. Say, for example, "For this reason I kneel before You, Father...." Use this passage to pray for the children and youth in your life, substituting your young person's name where applicable. Say, for example, "I pray that out of Your glorious riches You may strengthen Jennifer with power through Your Holy Spirit in her inner being." Conclude by praying those verses for yourself and your efforts to build stronger relationships with children and youth.

The Second Pillar

The second pillar in the process of passing on truth to children and youth is the pillar of example.

I have a friend named Frank; his son is called Frankie. Frank is a man of few words; so is his son. Frank appears the most comfortable when his hands are thrust into his pants pockets; Frankie is no different. Frank is a skilled mechanic; Frankie is fascinated by cars. Not once has his father ever explained or taught these behaviors to Frankie; but he has modeled them continually, without even thinking.

If you want to pass on biblical values to your children you must model those values in your own life. If you wish your teenage son or student or friend to accept the idea that there are absolute standards of right and wrong—that some things are right for all people, for all times, for all places—you must let them see that you believe it yourself.

I can think of nothing that is more detestable to a teenager than a hypocrite. And they believe there are a lot of them. In fact, only 29 percent of the youth participating in our survey could disagree with the statement, "There are a lot of hypocrites in my church."

Only 27 percent of our youth say their parents frequently "admit when they're wrong or mistaken." The study indicates that our children see our mistakes pretty clearly; what they seldom see are parents who are open and honest enough to admit their failures, seek forgiveness, and keep trying.

I am not saying that you must live a perfect life before your child—merely a consistent life, a life that models biblical standards (*Right From Wrong*, 127).

In addition to building a strong relationship with a young person, providing a good example is crucial if we expect to teach them anything about truth. It is not enough to *say* we believe in absolute truth; it is not even enough only to *believe* in absolute truth; we must admit, submit, *and* commit to following the truth. We must apply the truth to our own lives first. Remember, God said to Moses, "These commandments that I give you today are to be upon *your* hearts" first (Deuteronomy 6:6, emphasis added). Only after we take the commandments to heart can we effectively communicate the truth to the children and youth in our life.

A Well-Rounded Example

In his first letter to Timothy, the apostle Paul provides an outline that can systematically help us to confront the type of example we present to our loved ones.

Read 1 Timothy 4:9-12, noting particularly verse 12.

> [9]This is a trustworthy saying that deserves full acceptance [10](and for this we labor and strive), that we have put our hope in the living God, who is the Savior of all men, and especially of those who believe.
> [11]Command and teach these things. [12]Don't let anyone look down on you because you are young, but set an example for the believers in speech, in life, in love, in faith and in purity.

Paul admonishes Timothy not to let his youth deter him from passing on the truth by way of example. Which of the following do you think should deter us from striving to be good examples?

❑ past failures or shortcomings
❑ not knowing the Bible like we should
❑ gray hair
❑ personal insecurities
❑ fear
❑ the age of our kids
❑ other _____

In 1 Timothy 4:12, Paul identifies areas in which he exhorts Timothy to be an example. What are they? Circle them in the verse above.

What would have to change in *your* life for you to improve the example you set in ... (Be specific.)

...speech? _____

_____

...your daily life? _____

_____

...love? _____

_____

...faith?_____

_____

...purity? _____

_____

Self-Test

If you're having trouble discerning whether your example is all it should be, or identifying areas that need attention, the following self-test may help. Pause briefly before answering each question, and then answer as honestly and openly as you can.

• What is there in my life that I don't want others to know?

_____

• How has my behavior this week displayed my belief in absolute standards of morality?

_____

_____

• How has my behavior failed to display that belief? _____

_____

• Do I forbid behavior in children or youth that I allow in myself? If so, what?

_____

_____

• Am I open to criticism from others? _____

• Can I ask a child or teenager to help identify and correct inconsistent behavior in my life?

_____

• What divine precepts or principles do I resist or disobey?

_____

_____

Close today's study by praying the words of Psalm 139:23-24.

> Search me, O God, and know my heart; test me and know my anxious thoughts. See if there is any offensive way in me, and lead me in the way everlasting.

Follow with a prayer for the enabling power of God's Holy Spirit as you seek to build a relationship and be an example to the children and youth in your life.

The Third Pillar

How did you learn to ride a bicycle? Ice skate? Play the C-scale on a trombone? Drive a car? Bake a soufflé? Understand the opposite sex? (Oh, sorry; no one knows how to do that!)

Nonetheless, you probably learned such skills by having the task explained to you once, after which you climbed on your bicycle or put the trombone to your lips and—voilà!—you possessed a new skill, right? Well, no, probably not.

Chances are, if you can drive a car or bake a soufflé, you learned to do it by instruction. Often that instruction was repetitive.

Instilling biblical values in children and youth is no different. You cannot expect to explain the 4Cs once to a child or teenager and be done with it. You must talk about the process of discerning and following truth when you sit at home and when you walk along the road, when you lie down, and when you get up. The final pillar in the process of passing on truth to children and youth is sharing the truth—consistently, repeatedly, and at every opportunity.

Sharing the Truth

Take a few moments and meditate on the memory passage, Deuteronomy 6:6-7. Write it in the margin and repeat it three times. Then, answer the following questions.

Are the commandments of God (the precepts He has issued, the principles they reflect, and God's very nature on which they're based) on your heart? ❏ Yes ❏ Not as much I want them to be.

What practical steps can you take to "bind" God's ways upon your heart?

_____

In what ways can you begin now to share truth with children and youth "when you sit at home?" Remember that "home" doesn't have to be the place in which you live.

_____

_____

How can you begin now to share truth with youth "when you walk along the road?"

_____

_____

What would be the equivalent in your life of sharing truth with youth "when you lie down?"

_____

_____

In what ways can you share truth with youth "when you get up?"

_____

_____

Deuteronomy 6:8-9 instructs the people to "Tie them as symbols on your hands and bind them on your foreheads. Write them on the doorframes of your houses and on your gates."

The people of Israel were commanded to place potent reminders of God's truth in the way of their everyday activity, so that they would be reminded (when entering their house, for example) of God and His law. What can you do in your home, church, youth group, etc., to institute regular reminders of God and His truth?

_____

_____

Day by Day

"The tough thing about life," someone has said, "is that it's so daily." That's a fact. We never get a vacation from life; we can't get away from it. The laundry never stops piling up, the filing is never finished, the bills keep coming. It's the same with teaching children and youth the process of truth, helping them through the 4Cs, and reinforcing the evidence of God's protection and provision. It's so daily. It _must_ be daily. But it doesn't have to be difficult or painful.

Sharing the truth can be accomplished day by day, "when you sit at home," as the Scripture says, "and when you walk along the road." Take a few moments to work through the following list of opportunities, and imagine how you could share the truth with a young person in each situation. Write a brief description of what you might share.[1]

• Weddings and anniversaries _____

_____

• Television news broadcasts _____

_____

• Waiting in line to buy fast food _____

_____

• News of court trials and congressional hearings _____

_____

• Prime-time television series _____

_____

• The birth of a child in the family _____

_____

• Hearing a car alarm go off _____

_____

• Popular songs on the radios _____

_____

• Misplacing/finding a wedding ring _____

_____

• Graffiti on walls _____

_____

• A "bad" call by an umpire or referee _____

_____

• A disagreement between two friends or family members

_____

• Fences or barricades placed around dangerous sites _____

_____

• Waiting for a cake to rise _____

_____

• Making the bed together _____

_____

• Other _____

_____

Situations like those above don't necessarily call for a three-point sermon on the 4Cs, but they do present the opportunity for a word or two of reminder about the steps to truth. Perhaps also we would get a chance to ask a question that will lead a young person to recognize how God's protection and provision operates in many areas of our lives.

I like to take advantage of television shows, movies, even news broadcasts to teach truth—and consequences—to my children. From time to time the media does show negative consequences. For example, my son and I were watching a detective show in which two men sat at a bar; one purposefully lied to the other. That single lie got him wounded, jailed, and eventually cost him his family. When the show was over, I asked my son, "What can we learn from this? What were the consequences of lying?" We began a fruitful conversation about the Evidence of Truth.

I've used congressional hearings to discuss ethical matters with my children. I've used graffiti on walls to initiate a conversation that taught my children the Test of Truth. (*Right From Wrong*, 129-130).

Close today's study by reading 1 Timothy 2:3-4.

> This is good, and pleases God our Savior, who wants all
> men to be saved and to come to a knowledge of the truth.

Pray something like the following.

> *Father, I praise You because You are sovereign; I admit
> Your power as King over my life. I thank You for Your
> Word; I submit myself to Your precepts. I acknowledge
> that it is Your will that everyone be saved and come to a
> knowledge of the truth; I commit myself to that purpose.
> In the name of Jesus, the Way, the Truth, and the Life,
> amen.*

[1]See *Right From Wrong* for specific ideas in many of these areas.

Taking It to the Streets

A seventh-grader bows his head in the school cafeteria to pray a silent grace over his meal.

A university professor responds to a direct question by stating her conviction that homosexual behavior is immoral.

A mother tells a convenience store manager that she is offended by the prominent display of pornographic magazines by the cash register.

Each of these individuals, while they may be acting according to their convictions, are liable to be accused of intolerance, even bigotry.

That's because tolerance has arisen in our culture as a new cardinal virtue. Tolerance has become synonymous with goodness and open-mindedness; intolerance has come to connote bigotry. Many people think that Christians who talk about the truth (about God, Christ, or right and wrong) or pray politely in a public place are displaying intolerance toward those who do not agree with them.

Tolerance can be a good thing. Godly people give due consideration to people whose practices differ from their own; they are courteous and kind to those who don't view things the same way they do, refusing to judge anyone unkindly because God is the only one capable of judging righteously (see Psalm 9:3-10; Romans 14:10-13).

The fact that we are not to pass judgment on each other does not change the fact that truth is absolute. God's job is to judge; our job is to live according to His truth, and to share that truth in love and compassion.

Daniel's Stand

So how do we do that? It's one thing to communicate biblical truth to the children and youth in our family or church; but we are bound to face questions and challenges from educators, the media, our friends, neighbors, and colleagues. How do we take the truth to the streets? How do we "tell the truth" in our community? How do we balance absolute truth and appropriate tolerance?

Let's look at the example of Daniel, the Hebrew refugee who rose to prominence in Babylon.

What does Daniel 6:4 say about Daniel's character and behavior? Circle those characteristics in the verse below.

At this, the administrators and the satraps tried to find grounds for charges against Daniel in his conduct of government affairs, but they were unable to do so. They could find no corruption in him, because he was trustworthy and neither corrupt nor negligent.

Why is trustworthiness important for someone who is about to take a stand for truth?

_____

_____

Read verses 10-16, which describe how Daniel took a stand for truth.

[10]Now when Daniel learned that the decree had been published, he went home to his upstairs room where the windows opened toward Jerusalem. Three times a day he got down on his knees and prayed, giving thanks to his God, just as he had done before. [11]Then these men went as a group and found Daniel praying and asking God for help. [12]So they went to the king and spoke to him about his royal decree: "Did you not publish a decree that during the next thirty days anyone who prays to any god or man except to you, O king, would be thrown into the lions' den?"

The king answered, "The decree stands—in accordance with the laws of the Medes and Persians, which cannot be repealed."

[13]Then they said to the king, "Daniel, who is one of the exiles from Judah, pays no attention to you, O king, or to the decree you put in writing. He still prays three times a day." [14]When the king heard this, he was greatly distressed; he was determined to rescue Daniel and made every effort until sundown to save him.

[15]Then the men went as a group to the king and said to him, "Remember, O king, that according to the law of the Medes and Persians no decree or edict that the king issues can be changed."

[16]So the king gave the order, and they brought Daniel and threw him into the lions' den. The king said to Daniel, "May your God, whom you serve continually, rescue you!"

Which of the following words describe his behavior? Check all that apply.

❏ obnoxious	❏ resolute
❏ angry	❏ quiet
❏ determined	❏ confident
❏ bitter	❏ unkind
❏ disrespectful	❏ polite
❏ sarcastic	❏ wimpy
❏ haughty	❏ brave
❏ spiteful	❏ embarrassed

How did Daniel respond to the news that his beliefs and practices had been banned? (v. 11)

_____

_____

Was his behavior intolerant of the Babylonians' religions and customs?

❏ Yes, because _____

_____

❏ No, because _____

_____

Did Daniel know that standing for truth might bring unpleasant consequences? ❏ Yes ❏ No

Read Daniel 6:21-22 below.

21Daniel answered, "O king, live forever! 22My God sent his angel, and he shut the mouths of the lions. They have not hurt me, because I was found innocent in his sight. Nor have I ever done any wrong before you, O king."

How did Daniel treat the king after surviving a night with the lions? Check all that apply.

❏ disrespectfully	❏ angrily
❏ by praising God	❏ apologetically
❏ happily	❏ confidently
❏ bitterly	❏ unkindly
❏ respectfully	❏ politely
❏ sarcastically	❏ haughtily
❏ spitefully	❏ with dignity

Compare Daniel 6:16-17 to Daniel 6:23-26a, 28. What was the immediate effect of Daniel's stand for truth (vv. 16-17)? Underline your answer in the following verses.

> ¹⁶So the king gave the order, and they brought Daniel and threw him into the lions' den. The king said to Daniel, "May your God, whom you serve continually, rescue you!"
>
> ¹⁷A stone was brought and placed over the mouth of the den, and the king sealed it with his own signet ring and with the rings of his nobles, so that Daniel's situation might not be changed.

What was the eventual result of Daniel's stand for truth (vv. 23-26a, 28)?

> ²³The king was overjoyed and gave orders to lift Daniel out of the den. And when Daniel was lifted from the den, no wound was found on him, because he had trusted in his God.
>
> ²⁴At the king's command, the men who had falsely accused Daniel were brought in and thrown into the lions' den, along with their wives and children. And before they reached the floor of the den, the lions overpowered them and crushed all their bones.
>
> ²⁵Then King Darius wrote to all the peoples, nations and men of every language throughout the land:
>
> "May you prosper greatly!"
>
> ²⁶"I issue a decree that in every part of my kingdom people must fear and reverence the God of Daniel."
>
> ²⁸So Daniel prospered during the reign of Darius and the reign of Cyrus the Persian.

Your Stand for Truth

Using the items you checked in the lists on page 192 as a guide, what guidelines can you lay down to help you take a Daniel-like stand in a Babylonian-type culture? (For example, you may decide, "When I stand for truth, I will speak respectfully, act kindly ...") Write your guidelines below.

_____

_____

_____

_____

_____

Will that kind of behavior guarantee that you'll never be criticized or accused of being intolerant?

❑ Yes, because _____

❑ No, because _____

"Therefore," Paul wrote after discussing the kinds of things the Christian is up against in an often hostile culture, "put on the full armor of God, so that when the day of evil comes, you may be able to stand your ground, and after you have done everything, to stand" (Ephesians 6:13).

Stand for truth, then, unashamedly telling your family, friends, acquaintances, and community the truth about right and wrong, about how to make right choices, and about the loving God who longs to protect and provide for all of us.

You can do that with increasing effectiveness if you:
- Practice the 4Cs process for making right choices, relating this biblical process to the moral decisions you face. Remember always to:
    Consider the choice;
    Compare it to God;
    Commit to God's way; and
    Count on God's protection and provision.
- Encourage others to give thoughtful consideration to the choices they make (and the consequences that result).
- Use television shows, songs, news events, and other opportunities as springboards for discussing the 4Cs with the children and youth in your life.
- If your church has not already done so, encourage the implementation of the total Right From Wrong resources, which includes workbooks for all age levels, video series for youth and adults, and many other helpful components (see pages 9-12 for a list of available materials). The Right From Wrong resources will be most helpful and influential if used in a church-wide emphasis.
- Suggest that your group promote the showing of the *Truth Matters* five-part video series for adults. This series can be positioned as a church or community-wide event.
- Or your group can begin studying the workbook *Truth Matters* with a new group of adults, perhaps giving you and some of your fellow group members an opportunity to lead others.

Are You Ready?

Are you ready to make right choices? Are you ready to communicate biblical truth to the children and youth in your life? Are you ready to take it to the streets and take a godly stand for truth in your community? If you are, take a moment at the close of today's study to pray, perhaps using the following.

Dear Father, I praise You because You are the living God and You endure forever.

Help me to be like Daniel, who "was trustworthy and neither corrupt nor negligent" (Daniel 6:4).

Help me to be like Daniel, who stood for truth and trusted You to stand for him;

Help me to be like Daniel, who was not ashamed to tell the truth about You and Your commands, even when it meant facing lions;

Help me to be like Daniel,
who was not afraid to stand alone,
who was not afraid to stand for truth,
who was not afraid to stand on Your Word, amen.

WEEKLY JOURNAL

I learned that _____

_____

_____

One attitude I had which changed was _____

_____

_____

God spoke to me by _____

_____

_____

One behavior that I will examine is _____

_____

_____

When I shared with the child or youth in my life, _____

_____

_____

The most difficult thing was _____

_____

_____

It was a joy to _____

_____

_____

Tomorrow I will _____

_____

_____

My Scripture memory passage is _____

_____

WORKSHEETS FOR GROUP SESSIONS

The following pages contain the worksheets you will use during your weekly group sessions. Do not complete the worksheets until instructed to do so by your group leader. Take your workbook with you to group sessions because there is at least one worksheet for each session.

Every Day in America

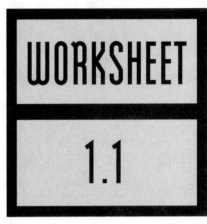

Research tells a statistical horror story of what is happening every day in America, a pattern that is reflected throughout our culture and around the world. Every day:

_____ unwed teenage girls become mothers

_____ teenage girls get abortions

_____ teenagers contract sexually transmitted diseases

_____ adolescents begin using drugs

_____ adolescents begin drinking alcohol

_____ pupils bring guns or other weapons to school

_____ teenagers are assaulted; _____ are raped

_____ teenagers drop out of high school

_____ teenagers commit suicide

(Statistics compiled from figures published by the Children's Defense Fund and the book, *13th Generation*, by Neil Howe and Bill Strauss)

What Can the Righteous Do?

Read Psalm 11:3, and discuss the following questions in your group.

What do you think David, the author of this psalm, might have been talking about when he talked about "the foundations" being destroyed?

_____

_____

_____

_____

Can you apply this verse to our day, to our culture, to our community, or to your family? Are there any "foundations" that you think are crumbling?

_____

_____

_____

_____

Does David answer his own question? If so, how? If not, why not?

_____

_____

_____

_____

How would you answer the question, "When the foundations are being destroyed, what can the righteous do?"

_____

_____

_____

Teach Me Your Ways

Look up Exodus 33:13, Moses' request to God after receiving the Law. Write the verse on the lines below.

_____

_____

_____

Have someone in your small group read the verse aloud. Then answer the following questions.

• Moses' words reveal that he had two goals. What were they?

1. _____

2. _____

• What did Moses want God to do to help him achieve those goals?

_____

_____

• What did Moses mean when he said, "teach me your ways?"

_____

_____

• How could learning God's ways help Moses to know God and find favor with Him?

_____

_____

• How could learning God's ways help us distinguish and defend right from wrong?

_____

The Truth Process

1. Define the three elements of the Truth Process by matching the description on the right with the term on the left.

Precept •   • nature and character of God

Principle •   • rules, regulations, codes, requirements of God

Person •   • norm or standard applicable to more than one situation

2. Place the three elements in the proper order in the Truth Process.

P _____   P _____   P _____

3. Making the right moral decisions results in God's

p _____ and p _____ .

Applying the 4Cs

#1 The phone rings. You answer and inform Heather that the call is for her. She asks you to "Say I'm not here." You refuse; Heather takes the call, but is mad because you refused to do her a simple favor.

- -

#2 Andrew's best friend missed two weeks of school because of "family problems." Now his friend wants Andy to help him out by writing a term paper for him—just this once—so he can make up his work. Andy figures he's just helping a friend.

- -

#3 Cheerleader Melissa's picture appeared in Saturday's paper, and she wants extra copies to send to relatives and friends. Late Saturday evening, you take her into town, put two quarters in the machine, and open the door. "There's a whole stack of papers in there," Melissa says. "Can we just take a couple extra? Nobody's going to buy any more papers tonight. They'll just go to waste otherwise."

- -

#4 Shaun, the star player on his soccer team of seven-year-olds, turns eight one week before the season starts, making him technically ineligible. The coach has listed his birthday incorrectly, making it possible for him to play if everyone just keeps quiet.

"The Court of Truth"

CASE #1 "I, Jeremy, the defendant, had two weeks to do a book report for school. I put off reading the book and played with my friends instead. The night before the report was due, I realized there was not enough time to read the book and do the report. I remembered that there is a movie about the book, though, so I rented the movie and watched it."

Walk Jeremy through the 4Cs.

_____

_____

- -

CASE #2 "I, Kelly, the defendant, and my friend were really thirsty and I only had enough money to buy one can of soda at the machine in the school cafeteria. I put the money in the soda machine; a can came out and my money came back in the coin return. I insisted on turning in the money at the school office, but now my friend's mad at me for making her share with me instead of buying her a can with the extra money."

Walk Kelly through the 4Cs.

_____

_____

- -

CASE #3 "I, Stephen, the defendant, was staying at home with my older sister. Our parents asked us to clean the house while they ran errands for three hours. While my parents were away, I watched TV while my sister cleaned. When my parents came home, they said, 'Thank you for making the house so beautiful. We are going to take you out for ice cream for doing all this hard work.' My sister glared at me, but did not say anything, although she had done all the work."

Walk Stephen through the 4Cs.

_____

_____

Love

Circle words and phrases in the following Scripture passage that define love.

Husbands, love your wives, just as Christ loved the church and gave himself up for her to make her holy, cleansing her by the washing with water through the word, and to present her to himself as a radiant church, without stain or wrinkle or any other blemish, but holy and blameless. In this same way, husbands ought to love their wives as their own bodies. He who loves his wife loves himself. After all, no one ever hated his own body, but he feeds and cares for it, just as Christ does the church (Ephesians 5:25-29).

According to God's Word, to love someone means to value their happiness, health, and spiritual growth as much as you do your own.

• If that's what love really is, what does that say about some of the things we call love?

_____

_____

_____

• If that's the kind of love God commands and values, how should submitting and committing to Him through the 4Cs process change the way we live? In your answer, offer specific, real-life examples.

_____

_____

_____

_____

_____

Three Role Plays

Follow these instructions if you are chosen to role play.

INSTRUCTIONS: Take a few moments to plan your role play together, deciding who will play each role and how you will act out the scene below. Try to create an appropriate ending for your scene: clever, funny, or challenging.

- -

ROLE PLAY #1
One of you is new at school, asking directions to study hall; the other must portray a person who clearly does not like you because of your hair color, eye color, accent, or clothes (pick one). The new student should respond patiently and respectfully to the other person's prejudice.

- -

ROLE PLAY #2
The two of you are talking about Tracy, one of the most popular girls at school, who also goes to church with both of you. One of you is extremely jealous; the other is proud that someone from your church is successful and popular in such a large school.

- -

ROLE PLAY #3
One of you is making fun of Linda, who has been teased because of her weight. The other expresses discomfort and regret over the way Linda is so often treated.

Churched Youth and Premarital Sex

Express your estimation of the actions and attitudes of church youth by marking each statement *T* (True) or *F* (False).

___ 1. More than 4 out of 10 churched youth today say that they would be more likely to have sexual intercourse if they were "in love with the other person."

___ 2. Four out of 10 churched youth say they would be more likely to have sexual intercourse with someone if they "really intended to marry" the other person.

___ 3. Churched youth who say they do not believe in absolute truth are four times more likely to have premarital sexual intercourse than youth who believe in absolute truth.

___ 4. Churched youth who do not believe in absolute truth are three times more likely to engage in "heavy petting" (fondling genitals) and two times more likely to fondle breasts than youth who believe in absolute truth.

___ 5. By age 18, more than one in four churched youth have had sexual intercourse.

Sexual Activity of Churched Kids [1]

ACTIVITY	% WHO HAVE ENGAGED IN ACTIVITY
Held hands	89%
Embracing & some kissing	81%
Heavy "French" kissing	53%
Fondling of breasts	34%
Fondling of genitals	26%
Sexual intercourse	16%

- -

Conditions Under Which Churched Youth Would Have Sexual Intercourse Today

Conditions	Conditions Make Intercourse:		
	More Likely	Less Likely	Doesn't Matter
You were in love with the person	46%	19%	36%
Really intended to marry them	44%	19%	37%
Positive a pregnancy would not result	26%	25%	49%
Knew your parents would not find out	26%	24%	51%
Felt your parents would not mind	22%	25%	54%
Friends strongly encouraged you to do so	11%	31%	58%

- -

Morally Acceptable Sexual Activity with Persons of the Opposite Sex, in Relation to the Respondent's Truth Views

(Base: said these activities are morally acceptable among unmarried, in love, consenting individuals.)

Conditions	Believe in absolute truth?	
	Yes	No
Holding hands	99%	99%
Embracing and some kissing	96%	97%
Heavy "French" kissing	73%	82%
Fondling of breasts	18%	37%
Fondling of genitals	11%	31%
Sexual intercourse	5%	21%

[1]All figures based on 1994 survey of 3,795 churched youth conducted for Right From Wrong campaign.

Choice Moments

1

"My boyfriend and I just had an argument. He wants to do more than just kiss on dates, and I'm afraid if I don't let him have his way, I'll lose him. In fact, he told me that there are plenty of girls who will let boys do what he wants to do. I think I really love him, so it wouldn't be so bad, would it?"

2

"My marriage has gone downhill for the last couple of years. I've grown really close to a woman at work. I'm not going to divorce my wife or anything, but a man needs some companionship once in a while, and I'm not getting it from my wife. I figure, if anything, I'd be *saving* my marriage by letting my friend at work meet some of the needs my wife can't—or won't. It can't be wrong for a man to save his marriage, can it?"

3

"We get FAO—the cable channel For Adults Only —and sometimes when my parents aren't home, I'll watch it. I figure there's nothing wrong with it. After all, I'm still a virgin and everything, I'm just watching stuff."

WORKSHEET

8.1

The Truth About Other Truths

Which issue will your "right from wrong" situation address?
(Circle one.)

JUSTICE   MERCY   RESPECT   SELF-CONTROL

What age child will be making this choice? (Circle one.)

PRESCHOOLER   ELEMENTARY-AGE CHILD   TEENAGER

Describe the hypothetical situation the young person is facing.

_____

_____

_____

Using the 4Cs process, guide the young person to choose right
instead of wrong.

- Step One is: _____
  How would you walk this person through Step One?

  _____

- Step Two is: _____
  What scriptural precepts would apply?

  _____

What scriptural principles would apply?

  _____

What attributes of God do those reflect?

  _____

- Step Three is: _____
  How would you walk this person through Step Three?

  _____

- Step Four is: _____
  What protections and provisions might result from committing to God's way in this choice?

  _____